Lotus® 1-2-3®

RELEASE 2.2

Bob Lewis, *Sheridan College*

Marianne Fox, *Butler University*
Lawrence Metzelaar, *Vincennes University*

Integrating computer-based instructional software developed by:

American Training International

 Addison-Wesley Publishers Limited

Don Mills, Ontario • Reading, Massachusetts
Menlo Park, California • New York • Wokingham, England
Amsterdam • Bonn • Sydney • Tokyo • Madrid • San Juan

Canadian Cataloguing in Publication Data

Lewis, Bob, 1946-
   Lotus 1-2-3, release 2.2

(Addison-Wesley computer-based learning series)
Includes Index.
ISBN 0-201-82198-2

1. Lotus 1-2-3 (Computer file). 2. Business -
Computer programs. 3. Electronic spreadsheets.
I. Fox, Marianne B. II. Metzelaar, Lawrence C.
III. Title. IV. Series.

HF5548.4.L67L48 1994   650′.0285′5369   C94-931722-5

ISBN 0-201-82198-2

Printed in Canada.

A B C D E WC 98 97 96 95 94

TRADEMARKS

CONTENTS

INTRODUCTION

TO THE *BASIS* MODULES

The Basic Academic Skills - Independent Study (*BASIS*) system is designed to help you develop some of the foundation skills you will need in your post-secondary training and in your future career.

Computers are playing an ever-increasing role in the workplace, and the *BASIS* Computer Applications series of modules emphasizes the skills most in demand.

All *BASIS* modules have the same format:

> STEP 1   Computer-based tutorials
>
> STEP 2   Structured practice exercises
>
> STEP 3   Competency testing

BASIS modules are easy to use. You start with the computer-based tutorial, work your way through related practice exercises, then do the competency test when scheduled. A Class Assistant[1] is available during all scheduled lab classes to help out with individual problems, check off progress, and administer tests.

Before you start the *BASIS* module, it is very important that you read through the introductory material which begins below.

Welcome to the *BASIS* system, and good luck!

---

[1] The term "Class Assistant" is used throughout to designate the person available during scheduled class time to check off completed work, etc. Your institution may refer to this person in another way.

FORM

All *BASIS* modules follow the same format:

- Every module is divided into major topics.

  Each major topic starts with a box exactly like the one on page 1.

- Each topic contains four sections:

  - Topic Objectives

  - Computer Tutorial

  - Practice Exercises

  - Competency Testing

These sections are identified by the following icons:

 TOPIC OBJECTIVES

 COMPUTER TUTORIAL

 PRACTICE EXERCISES

 COMPETENCY TESTING

The sections are laid out in a logical and carefully designed sequence. *We strongly recommend that you do work in the order in which it is presented in modules.* Skipping around may lead to confusion and/or unnecessary mistakes, both of which are needlessly time-consuming. You will detect some repetition of specific tasks between sections. This is intentional: skills are only learned and developed by practice.

Pages ix and x outline the four sections in greater detail.

Sections Within Each Topic

 ## Topic Objectives

Every major topic in a *BASIS* module begins with a list of topic objectives. *You should always read the topic objectives before beginning a major topic.*

Topic objectives outline for you:

- What you should learn from working through the topic.

- What you should expect to be able to demonstrate on the competency test.

The **Topic Objectives** section within each major topic outlines for you exactly what the objectives are for that major topic.

 ## Computer Tutorial

BASIS computer tutorials take you through material that shows you how to meet each of the objectives outlined in the Topic Objectives.

The computer tutorials are interactive: you just follow on-screen explanations and instructions, then enter information or press various keys when you're asked to do so. The tutorial program won't let you press the wrong buttons, so don't worry about making mistakes. The computer tutorials often include practice exercises, and always review all material covered.

The computer tutorials provide the major instruction for all *BASIS* modules. Therefore, in order to be fully prepared for the competency test for that module, it is your responsibility to:

- Do all assigned computer tutorial material.

- Do all recommended practice material within the computer tutorial.

- Make notes for yourself where you feel it is necessary for you to do so to fully understand the material covered.

- Repeat material you do not understand the first time.

The **Computer Tutorial** section within each major topic outlines for you exactly which parts of the computer tutorial you are supposed to do for that major topic.

PRACTICE EXERCISES

Practice exercises help you strengthen your understanding of concepts covered in the related computer tutorial. In a few instances, explanatory material will be introduced in the Practice Exercises section only and not in the computer tutorial. On those occasions when objectives are met through material in only one place (the computer tutorial or the practice exercises), that fact will be highlighted in the Topic Objectives.

There are three parts to the practice exercises for each major topic:

- **PROJECTS**   A series of small, specific projects written as command-based instruction. These projects, together, lead to completion of a larger project.

- **STUDY QUESTIONS**   Short true/false and fill-in the blanks exercises to be used as self-tests to help you measure your progress.

- **REVIEW EXERCISES**   Hands-on tasks with numbered steps. These "abbreviated" instructions (without specific commands shown) help you build on skills learned in the topic without "leading" you step by step.

The **Practice Exercises** section within each major topic outlines for you exactly which projects, study questions, and review exercises you are supposed to do for that major topic.

COMPETENCY TESTING

The competency test for each *BASIS* module is a comprehensive, hands-on test of approximately 45 to 60 minutes duration. (There may be a short written portion on Windows in the test for the DOS and Windows modules.) It is designed to measure your competency with respect to *all topic objectives combined.*

In order to qualify to write the competency test for any given *BASIS* module, you must have completed *all* practice exercises associated with *all* topics for that module.

The **Competency Testing** section within each major topic outlines for you exactly which projects, study questions, and review exercises you must have "checked off" by your Class Assistant for that major topic in order to qualify to write the competency test for the module.

INTRODUCTION TO LOTUS 1-2-3, RELEASE 2.2

hile word processing programs are used to manipulate text data, electronic spreadsheets aid in the manipulation of numerical data. Electronic spreadsheets like Lotus 1-2-3 are simply automated versions of the lined ledger sheet used in accounting. In fact, any time you work with numbers in rows and columns on a piece of paper, you could make your job much easier and more efficient using a product like Lotus 1-2-3.

Like a word processing program, an electronic spreadsheet makes changing, moving, copying or deleting entries easier, but far more valuable is its ability to rapidly and automatically perform the necessary recalculations following this editing. As with word processing program documents, spreadsheet data can be appropriately formatted with numbers appearing as percentages, dollars or whatever is needed. Spreadsheets include a number of unique and powerful features including a variety of built-in formulas to perform both routine (e.g., addition) and sophisticated (e.g., statistical) operations automatically, but their most powerful capacity is the facility for "what-if" analysis. A retail owner can change the value for profit margin, for example, and in the wink of an eye, see the effect on the "bottom line". Finally, the ability to represent spreadsheet data and calculations graphically makes spreadsheets especially useful in developing effective material for presentations.

GETTING STARTED

In this *BASIS* computer applications module for **Lotus 1-2-3**, you will develop many of the skills outlined above. You will remember from the introductory section that within every topic in a *BASIS* module there are four sections: Topic Objectives, Computer Tutorial, Practice Exercises, and Competency Testing. *If you have not read the explanation of these four sections, please do so now before continuing further* (see **Introduction to the *BASIS* Modules**, pages v to viii).

First read the Topic Objectives, then start the computer tutorial. Take notes when necessary to fully understand the material. After you finish the computer tutorial sections indicated, work through the practice exercises. Finally, read the Competency Testing outline carefully since it summarizes the work you must have completed from the topic to qualify for the competency test at the end of the module.

TOPIC OBJECTIVES

As explained in the **Introduction to the *BASIS* Modules**, every major topic in a *BASIS* module begins with a list of topic objectives which outline for you:

- What you should learn from working through the topic.

- What you should expect to be able to demonstrate on the competency test.

In this **Introduction to Lotus 1-2-3** topic, you will learn how to:

- Start Lotus 1-2-3.

- Perform basic file maintenance tasks.

  - Set directory temporarily.

  - Save current worksheet.

  - Erase worksheet and begin creating a new worksheet.

  - Retrieve a file from disk.

- Move around worksheet (special keys).

- Select option from a menu.

  - Access the Lotus 1-2-3 menu system.

- Use function keys.

  - Ten function keys.

  - Edit keys.

- Use Lotus 1-2-3's on-line help facility.

- Display Access System menu (*Note*: Covered in Computer Tutorial *only*).

- Exit Lotus.

- Understand the worksheet screen.

COMPUTER TUTORIAL

The sections from the Lotus Tutorial listed below are to be covered for this **Introduction to Lotus 1-2-3** topic.

- Select the *BASIS* **Lotus 1-2-3 Tutorial** in the manner indicated by your *BASIS* System Administrator[2] and/or your *BASIS* **Student Manual**.[3]

---

[2] The term System Administrator is used throughout to designate the person responsible for management of the *BASIS* system where you are using it. Your institution may refer to this person in another way.

[3] A *BASIS* Student Manual may not be used at all institutions and/or another term may be used to refer to it at your institution.

- From the **Novice** section, work through:

  A How to use your training program

  B Getting started with Lotus 1-2-3

  D Enter data

  N Exit to DOS (skip section on Add-Ins or treat as optional)

NOTE

- Be sure to use the bookmark feature.

  It will be very helpful to you, showing you what you have completed, and bringing you back at the right place when you resume work that you have interrupted.

  In addition, to qualify you to attempt the competency test at the end of this module, you must have covered the required work. This will be checked, in part, by examining bookmark references on your disk.

- You may not be starting Lotus 1-2-3 in the way outlined in the tutorial. Be sure to start Lotus 1-2-3 in the manner indicated by your *BASIS* System Administrator and/or your *BASIS* **Student Manual**.

  Information on starting Lotus 1-2-3 from the DOS prompt is included in this *BASIS* module even though that may not be the case at your institution because that is the way you may start applications in many other environments (future jobs, for example).

 ## PRACTICE EXERCISES

If this is the first BASIS module you have used, be sure you have read through the introductory section at the beginning of this book for an explanation of the way the module is organized.

In all Practice Exercises in this module (*except* this one), you must print a "topic directory listing" showing files on your data diskette after completing *all* Practice Exercise work (including Review Exercises). Do this in the manner indicated by your *BASIS* System Administrator and/or your *BASIS* **Student Manual**.

The practice exercise activities for the **Introduction to Lotus 1-2-3** topic are:

- Read pages 4 to 13. Make notes in the margins and/or highlight material as you go where you find it necessary to do so to fully understand the material covered. The **Key Terms** and **Summary** sections are especially helpful. (There is no keyboard work in this practice exercise section.)

- Do **True/False** exercises on page 14.

- Do **Fill in the Blanks** exercises on page 14.

NOTE

- As previously indicated in the NOTE with the Computer Tutorial, you may not be starting Lotus 1-2-3 in the way outlined on page 4. Be sure to start Lotus 1-2-3 in the manner indicated by your *BASIS* System Administrator and/or your *BASIS* **Student Manual**.

STARTING LOTUS 1-2-3

To access Lotus 1-2-3, follow the appropriate method described below.

➤ To start Lotus 1-2-3 on a dual floppy-disk system:

1. Access the DOS A> prompt.

2. Remove the boot disk and insert the Lotus System disk into drive A:.

3. Insert a blank formatted data disk into drive B:.

4. At the A> prompt, type **123** and press ⏎.

   A blank worksheet containing columns A through H and rows 1 through 20 appears after a copyright message. The word "READY" appears in the upper-right corner of the screen.

➤ To start Lotus 1-2-3 on a hard disk system:

1. Follow the procedures for your system that will load Lotus 1-2-3 and present the initial blank worksheet displaying columns A through H and rows 1 through 20. The word "READY" appears in the upper-left corner of the screen.

2. Once you begin this module, you will create and save new files or retrieve existing files. If you fail to specify a disk drive when saving or retrieving files, Lotus 1-2-3 uses the current directory. At the end of each session, you can exit the current worksheet and begin working with another, or return to DOS.

UNDERSTANDING BASIC FILE MAINTENANCE TASKS

Following is a brief summary of the most common file maintenance tasks that you will use in the projects that follow. Before you start a command sequence, "READY" must appear as the mode indicator in the upper-right corner of the Lotus 1-2-3 screen.

Do not perform these steps now, because they will be discussed in detail in subsequent sections. If you forget how to perform a basic task when working with your own applications, refer to this section.

➤ To temporarily set the current directory:

1. Press / to activate the Main menu.

2. Press **F** to access the File menu.

3. Press **D** to access the current **D**irectory option.

4. Type the letter of the disk drive followed by a colon (:).

5. Type the subdirectory path (hard disk users only).

6. Press ⏎.

Sample current directories include A: (hard disk users storing files on drive A:), C:\123\DATA (hard disk users storing files on the Lotus 1-2-3 data subdirectory), and B: (dual floppy-disk users storing files on drive B:). If you are using this module in a classroom environment, your instructor will specify the current directory appropriate to the equipment in use.

➤ To save the current worksheet to disk:

1. Press / to access the Main menu.

2. Press **F** to access the **F**ile menu.

3. Press **S** to access the **S**ave option.

4. Check that the correct path appears in the Control Panel at the top of the screen. If incorrect, press [Esc] a sufficient number of times to clear the unwanted portion, and then type the correct drive\directory\path.

5. Type the file name you want to use to store the worksheet on disk.

6. Press [↵].

If the file you are using already exists on disk, you will see a message prompting you to **C**ancel the Save command, **R**eplace the file on disk with the current file in memory, or **B**ackup the old file on disk before saving the new worksheet. Select **R**eplace to update the file on disk.

If you have not saved changes to the current worksheet, before exiting you will see a warning message in the Control Panel. Select **Y**es again to complete the exit process or select **N**o to abort the exit in order to first save the worksheet.

For example, you can save a file developed in this module by giving it the name of the last page you completed, such as PAGE89. This way you can return to where you stopped or repeat portions of the lesson to reinforce a concept.

Caution: As you create or edit a file, save your work periodically. Lotus 1-2-3 does not have an automatic Save feature, and a power interruption will destroy all changes made to the file since the last time it was saved.

➤ To erase the current worksheet and begin creating a new worksheet:

1. Press / to access the Main menu.

2. Press **W** to access the **W**orksheet submenu.

3. Press **E** to **E**rase the current worksheet from memory.

4. Press **Y** to confirm the erasure. (Selecting **N**o cancels the erasure.)

    Erasing the worksheet from memory does not destroy the version stored on disk.

➤ To retrieve a file from disk:

1. Press / to activate the Main menu.

2. Press **F** to access the **F**ile menu.

3. Press **R** to access the **R**etrieve option.

    Type the file name you want to retrieve and press [↵].

    You can also use [→] and [←] to highlight the name of the file to be retrieved from memory and press [↵].

WORKSHEET BASICS

This section will orient you to working in Lotus 1-2-3. You will find additional information in the manuals that come with your software, and in the numerous reference books and periodicals available in libraries and bookstores. Ask your instructor or another technical resource person to suggest additional readings.

Read this section carefully. An understanding of the Lotus 1-2-3 screen format and keyboard is essential. In the projects in this module, you will use the information summarized here as you follow the detailed hands-on instructions. Refer to this section for assistance as necessary.

THE WORKSHEET SCREEN

When you access Lotus 1-2-3, you see the blank *worksheet* screen shown in the following figure.

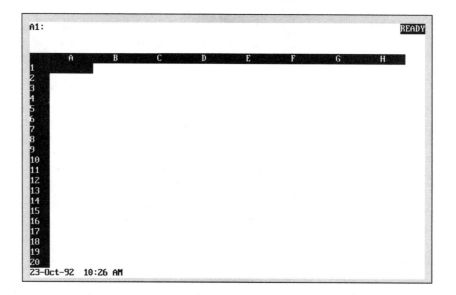

Instead of the neatly ruled rows and columns you find on ledger paper, you see black border areas that contain row numbers and column letters. Important information about the status of Lotus 1-2-3 appears at the top and bottom of the screen. This information continually changes as you use the program.

Refer to the following figure as you read subsequent descriptions.

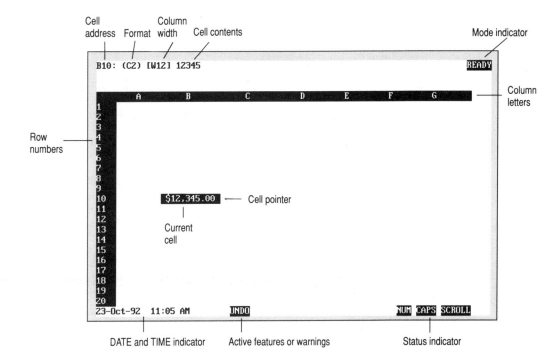

COLUMN LETTERS AND ROW NUMBERS

The intersection of individual column letters and row numbers form the address, or coordinates, of each Lotus 1-2-3 *cell*. Notice that the highlighted cell formed by the intersection of column B and row 10 is described by coordinates in the upper-left corner of the screen, "B10:." Rows are numbered 1 through 8192 and columns are lettered A through IV (totaling 256). Although there is potential for 2,097,152 cells in a single worksheet, the number of cells you can actually use depends on how much memory is in the computer. Because an entire worksheet is placed in memory at one time, the size of your actual worksheet is limited to the amount of memory available after DOS and Lotus 1-2-3 are loaded.

CELLS AND CELL ADDRESSES

As explained above, each individual *cell* is identified by its column letter and row number, which constitute the ***cell address.*** For example, the first cell in column A is A1; the fifth cell in column L is L5; the seventh cell in column AB is AB7, or in column IL, IL7. Although it is theoretically possible, it is unlikely that your worksheet will reach cell IV8192.

MODE INDICATORS, ACTIVE FEATURES, AND STATUS INDICATORS

In the upper-right corner of the screen, the ***mode indicator*** shows the *mode* that Lotus 1-2-3 is in at the moment. A few modes are outlined next. Watch for others as you work through the projects. Refer to the Lotus 1-2-3 reference manual for a complete listing.

READY	Data can be entered in the worksheet.
MENU	Selection from menus is required.
POINT	Specification of a group of cells is required.

An active feature, or warning, is shown at the bottom of the screen. In the figure, notice UNDO, indicating that the Undo feature is active or turned on. The Undo feature, new to Releases 2.2 and 3.0, allows you to erase (or undo) the last command performed by pressing [Alt]-[F4].

In the lower-right corner of the screen, *status indicators* display the *status* of certain toggle keys:

CAPS	Displays when the [caps lock] key is pressed. Alphabetic characters appear in uppercase instead of the usual lowercase.
NUM	Displays when the [Num Lock] key is pressed. The numeric keyboard is activated.
SCROLL	Displays when the [Scroll Lock] key is pressed. The window on the screen moves (scrolls) each time the cell pointer is moved.

In the middle of the bottom line on the screen, you may also see either of these two status indicators:

| CIRC | Displays if your worksheet contains a formula that refers to itself (CIRCular reference, usually a design flaw). |
| CALC | Displays if you change cell content that influences a formula when your mode of recalculation is manual (the default mode is automatic). |

DATE AND TIME INDICATOR

In the lower-left corner of the screen, the current date and time are displayed. If you are using Release 2.2 or higher, you can display either the date and time or the name of the current worksheet in memory. As necessary, various messages momentarily replace the current date and time. Messages such as "Printer error" or "Protected cell" usually indicate that an error has occurred and needs attention. When an error appears in this area, the mode indicator will show ERROR.

THE CELL POINTER AT THE CURRENT CELL

The highlighted area at the B10 position is known as the *cell pointer*. As the cell pointer is moved to other locations, the cell information area in the Control Panel is updated to indicate the contents of each new cell.

THE CONTROL PANEL

The Control Panel is a dynamic work area used by Lotus 1-2-3 to communicate with the user. It consists of three lines at the top of the screen, above the worksheet column heading. Line 1 contains cell and worksheet status information. Lines 2 and 3 display characters being entered or edited, menus, and explanations of menu items highlighted.

In the previous figure, "B10:" in line 1 is the address of the cell where the cell pointer is currently located. Notice that cell B10 is highlighted. "(C2)" indicates that cell B10 has been set to Currency format with two decimal places displayed. The column width, "[W12]," indicates that column B has been set to accept 12 characters. The entry "12345" reports the contents of the current cell, B10. When a cell contains a formula instead of a number or label, the results of the formula are displayed in the worksheet, but the formula itself is shown on line 1 of the Control Panel.

When an entry is being created or edited, it is displayed on line 2 of the Control Panel. If you press slash (/) in READY mode, the Main menu appears. Prompts or requests for additional information for completing a command are displayed here.

Line 3 displays either submenus or a description of the command currently highlighted on the menu.

THE KEYBOARD

Before you begin to create your own worksheets, databases, and graphs, you should understand the keyboard as it applies to Lotus 1-2-3. The following tables summarize most of the cursor movement and menu keystrokes you will be using.

POINTER MOVEMENT KEYS

If the arrow and number keys are on the same keypad, press ⎀[Num Lock] to turn off numbers and activate the cursor movement keys. If the keyboard includes a separate keypad containing the cell pointer keys, you do not have to turn off [Num Lock].

[↓] [←] [→] [↑]	Move the cell pointer one cell down, left, right, or up, respectively.
[Home]	Moves the cell pointer to cell A1 (the upper-left cell of the worksheet).
[End]	Used in combination with one of the four arrow keys, moves the cell pointer to the top, bottom, left, or right area of the worksheet indicated. [End]-[Home] moves the cell pointer to the bottom-right corner of the current worksheet.
[PgUp]	Moves the cell pointer up one screen at a time (20 rows).
[PgDn]	Moves the cell pointer down one screen at a time (20 rows).
[Ctrl]	Used in combination with [←] or [→], moves the cell pointer one screen at a time left or right. The number of columns moved depends on the width of the columns displayed.

MENU KEYS

You must press certain keys to access the Lotus 1-2-3 menu system and complete a menu selection. At any point during the process of executing a command sequence, you can abort all or part of the menu selections.

/	Activates the Lotus 1-2-3 Main command menu. (Don't confuse the forward slash with the backslash \. The backslash fills a cell with the character(s) that follows *or* names a macro when used with a letter of the alphabet.)
⏎	Selects the highlighted menu option or confirms your choice of information to Lotus 1-2-3, such as selecting a file for retrieval, specifying a range of cells, or indicating a number of decimal places.
Esc	Backs out of a command sequence one level for each time the key is pressed. Also used to leave status screen displays or to exit the EDIT mode without making changes.

FUNCTION KEYS

The IBM PC keyboard has ten function keys located either at the left side or across the top of the keyboard. With Lotus 1-2-3, the function keys perform the following operations:

F1	Help	Suspends the current Lotus 1-2-3 operation and produces the Help display on the screen.
F2	Edit	Displays the contents of the current cell in the Control Panel so they can be edited.
F3	Name	While in POINT mode only, displays a menu of range names.
F4	Abs	While in POINT and EDIT modes, causes the cell addresses to be absolute or not absolute (see Project 2).
F5	GoTo	Moves the cell pointer to any cell in the worksheet indicated by the user.
F6	Window	While a split screen is in effect, toggles the cell pointer between the split portions.
F7	Query	Causes the most recent Data Query command sequence to be repeated.
F8	Table	Causes the most recent Data Table command sequence to be repeated.
F9	Calc	While in READY mode, recalculates the worksheet. While in VALUE or EDIT mode, converts the formula in a cell to the current value.

| [F10] | Graph | Causes a graph to be drawn according to the most recent specifications. |

FUNCTION KEY COMBINATIONS

The combination of [Alt] and function keys listed next supports features available with Lotus 1-2-3 Releases 2.2 and 3.0 or higher only.

[Alt]-[F1]	Compose	Creates special nonkeyboard characters.
[Alt]-[F2]	Step	Finds errors in macro programs.
[Alt]-[F3]	Run	Executes a macro program.
[Alt]-[F4]	Undo	Reverses the last action made to the worksheet.
[Alt]-[F5]	Learn	When turned on, saves the next 512 keystrokes into a cell; they can then be executed, saving typing time and errors when creating macros.
[Alt]-[F7]	APP1	Starts an application developed to work with this key.
[Alt]-[F8]	APP2	Starts an application developed to work with this key.
[Alt]-[F9]	APP3	Starts an application developed to work with this key.
[Alt]-[F10]	Add-in	Accesses the ADD-IN manager.

EDIT KEYS

While in EDIT mode, you can use the keys listed below to execute the actions indicated.

[←]		Moves the cursor one character to the left.
[→]		Moves the cursor one character to the right.
[Ctrl]-[←]		Moves the cursor five characters to the left.
[Ctrl]-[→]		Moves the cursor five characters to the right.
[Home]		Moves the cursor to the first character in the line.
[End]		Moves the cursor to the last character in the line.
[Del]		Deletes the character in the current cursor position.
[Backspace]		Deletes the character preceding the cursor.
[Ins]		Toggles between the default INSERT mode and the alternate OVERSTRIKE mode. If OVERSTRIKE is active, OVR appears as a status indicator.

Getting Help

Lotus 1-2-3 provides on-screen Help when you press F1. Pressing F1 in READY mode displays a 1-2-3 Help Index, from which you can view information about a variety of topics. When a menu option is highlighted on the current screen, press F1 to display information about that command. The help is *context-sensitive*, which means that the information you see varies according to the command in progress at the time the Help key is pressed. The following figure illustrates the Help screen that appears if F1 is pressed after initiating a command to change column width.

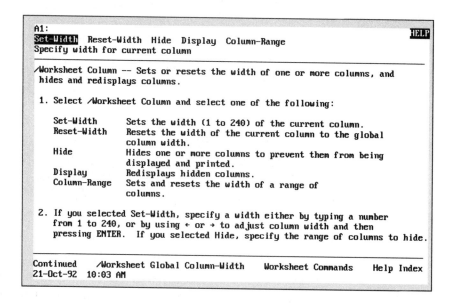

➤ **To display the 1-2-3 Help Index:**

1. Check that a blank worksheet in READY mode appears on your screen.

2. Press F1.

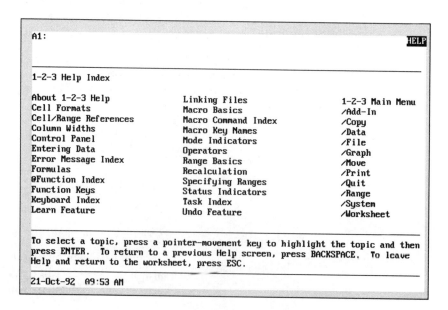

3. Press ⏎ to display information on "About 1-2-3 Help."

4. After reading the general description about the Help feature, press Esc to return to the worksheet.

EXITING LOTUS 1-2-3

The last item on many Lotus 1-2-3 menus is an option to quit or exit the current application. To exit the program, select **/Q**uit **Y**es. If you are using version 2.2 or higher, you will see an additional message if you have not saved changes to the current worksheet, as shown in the next figure.

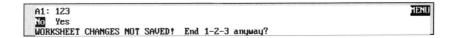

SUMMARY

- Lotus 1-2-3 is an integrated software package offering three applications: worksheet, *graphics*, and *database* management.

- Each Lotus 1-2-3 worksheet contains 256 columns and 8192 rows. Rows are numbered 1 through 8192; columns are lettered A through Z, AA through AZ, BA through BZ, CA through CZ, and so on until the last column, IV.

- The intersection of a column and a row is a cell. A cell pointer highlights the current cell.

- A variety of indicators appears in the corners of the screen: date and time, mode, and status. Information about other active features may appear on occasion in the middle of the status line at the bottom of the screen.

- A three-line Control Panel appears above the worksheet work surface. Line 1 contains cell and worksheet status information. Lines 2 and 3 display characters being entered or edited, menus, and explanations of menu items highlighted.

- Lotus 1-2-3 provides a variety of keys to press as you enter, edit, or view data and execute commands: pointer movement keys, menu keys, function keys, and function key combinations.

- Pressing F1 accesses the Help facility. Pressing the key when READY mode is active causes the Lotus 1-2-3 Help Index to appear. If you press the key during specification of a Lotus 1-2-3 command, context-sensitive information appears.

KEY TERMS

cell	context-sensitive	mode indicator
cell address	database	status indicator
cell pointer	graphics	worksheet
combination keys		

STUDY QUESTIONS

TRUE/FALSE

1. The Control Panel displays status indicators NUM, CAPS, and SCROLL. **(T)** **F**

2. Column letters and row numbers combine to form the address of each Lotus 1-2-3 cell. **(T)** **F**

3. Cell information that appears in the Control Panel includes, but is not limited to, the current address of the cell pointer and the contents of the cell highlighted by the cell pointer. **(T)** **F**

4. Press [Home] to move the cell pointer to cell A1. **(T)** **F**

5. Press [Ctrl]-[→] to move the cell pointer to the far-right end of the worksheet. **(T)** **F**

6. Press / to access the main Lotus 1-2-3 menu. **(T)** **F**

7. Press [F2] to access on-line Help. **T** **(F)**

8. The mode indicator READY means that you can enter data in the worksheet. **T** **F**

9. To exit Lotus 1-2-3, press [Esc] until the DOS prompt appears. **T** **(F)**

10. The Control Panel occupies the first three rows of the worksheet. **(T)** **F**

FILL IN THE BLANKS

1. When data can be entered in the worksheet, the mode indicator displays _____.

2. To move the cell pointer to cell A1, press __Home__.

3. The cell highlighted by the cell pointer is called the __current__ cell.

4. To access the Main menu, press ___/___.

5. The date and time are normally displayed in the __BTm/LEFT__ corner of the screen.

6. To move the cell pointer up 20 rows, press __PGUP__.

7. The indicators in the lower-right corner of the screen indicate the status of certain __Edit__ keys.

8. The _____ indicator at the bottom of the screen indicates that a formula refers to itself, usually a design flaw.

9. Press __F1__ to access on-line Help.

10. When you press the slash (/) key, the mode indicator displays __menu__.

COMPETENCY TESTING

- Review the Topic Objectives to ensure you have mastered all skills listed.

- Ask your Class Assistant to check off your completed True/False and Fill in the Blanks exercises.

- Ask your Class Assistant to see the **True/False and Fill in the Blanks Correct Answer Sheet** for this topic and compare your answers against the correct ones.

CREATING A WORKSHEET

TOPIC OBJECTIVES

After completing this topic, you should be able to:

- Design a worksheet.

- Enter labels, numbers, formulas, and functions.

- Edit data.

- Change column width.

  - Change single column.

  - Change global width.

- Specify number formats (range or global).

- Save, print, and erase current worksheet.

- Cancel (undo) most recent change (*Note*: Covered in Computer Tutorial *only*).

COMPUTER TUTORIAL

- From the **Novice** section, work through:

  C Create a worksheet

  D Enter data (as a review, if necessary; done last topic)

  F Save your work

  G Perform calculations (half of option G, as follows):

    - Enter a formula

    - Format a range of cells

    - Specify a range by highlighting cells

  M Print with Lotus 1-2-3 (only first item in option M, as follows):

    - Print a range of cells

- From the **Advanced** section, work through:

  A Set up an inventory worksheet

PRACTICE EXERCISES

- Read and complete all **Project 1 work** outlined on pages 18 to 31:

  - Take special note of the **Key Terms** and **Summary** sections.

  - Be sure to save the worksheet **SAMPLE** (see also NOTE, below).

  - Be sure to keep the printout (page 30).

- Do **True/False** exercises on page 31.

- Do **Fill in the Blanks** exercises on page 32.

- Do all **Review Exercises** on pages 32 and 33, entering your name next to *"Prepared by:"*, and saving the worksheet as **PERSPROP**.

- Do the required **Topic Directory Listing** (**TDL**). If you've forgotten, see **Introduction to Lotus 1-2-3** topic: Practice Exercises section for an explanation.

NOTE

- You may not need to indicate drive when you save files. The Lotus 1-2-3 you're using may automatically save files to the drive into which you have inserted your data diskette. If the system you are using "defaults" to this drive, it is not necessary to specify a different path, as described in the third paragraph on page 27.

- Understanding the differences between the three types of data that worksheet cells may contain [labels, numbers, and formulas (or functions)] is very important.

  After reading pages 19 and 20, be sure you know how labels, numbers, and formulas (or functions) differ.

  A very common *mistake* is to insert one of the label prefixes in front of a number, thereby *changing it to a label*. Lotus 1-2-3 automatically right-aligns numbers and *you cannot change this*. New users often try putting a caret (^) in front of numbers in a column thinking that will center the numbers. While the results do appear centered, they have also been changed to labels by the caret and can therefore no longer have mathematical operations performed on them. The bottom line: *don't try to align numbers*: Lotus 1-2-3 does it automatically (and only) to the right.

- It is also very important that you understand how to change the format of the display of numeric data. To show numbers with dollar signs or percentage signs, for example, you do *not* enter these signs as data. Instead, you "format" the numbers to appear with the dollar sign or percentage sign (or whatever you prefer). Be sure to pay close attention to the section "Specifying Number Formats" on pages 25 to 27.

PROJECT 1: CREATING A WORKSHEET

DESIGNING THE WORKSHEET

Creating a condensed Income Statement for a single month, as shown in the following figure, provides an introduction to several concepts. Study the worksheet you are about to create. The model in the figure contains label data, numbers, and formulas.

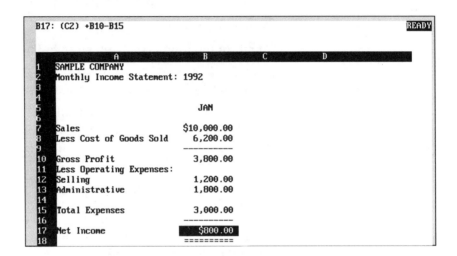

Columns A and B in the figure contain headings, account titles, and separator lines. These non-numeric cell entries are all called *label* data. The heading "Monthly Income Statement: 1992" is referred to as a *long label*. A long label exceeds the width of the column in which it is stored. If no data is stored in the adjacent cell on the right, the label displays into the next column. However, if the adjacent cell contains data, the excess part of the label entry is hidden from view. It is important to note that when excess data is hidden from view, it is not lost. The entire entry can be seen in line 1 of the Control Panel, or if the adjacent cell is erased, the long label can be seen on the worksheet again.

The figures in column B for "Sales," "Cost of Goods Sold," "Selling," and "Administrative" expenses are entered as *numbers*. The figures in column B for "Gross Profit," "Total Expenses," and "Net Income" result from entering *formulas*.

In the upper-right corner of the Control Panel, READY indicates that you can enter and edit data in the worksheet. Information about the currently highlighted cell in the worksheet appears in the first line of the Control Panel. The following information is displayed about cell B17:

- (C2) indicates that cell B17 has been formatted to display numbers in currency to two decimal places.

- +B10–B15 is the actual content of cell B17, not the $800.00 result displayed in the worksheet. +B10–B15 is the formula that subtracts the contents of cell B15 from the contents of cell B10 (Gross Profit minus Total Expenses).

The initial worksheet model for this module has been designed for you. However, when you create a worksheet of your own, you should first have a

design in mind for the placement of the labels, numbers ⌐
want to enter. Carefully planning the design, and sketching
worksheet on paper, can save you considerable editing time in ⌐
electronic worksheet.

Now that you understand the worksheet area and Control Panel, the purpoⲧ
of selected keystrokes, and the design of the initial model, you can access
Lotus 1-2-3 and begin the hands-on exercises in this project.

TYPES OF DATA

Worksheet cells may contain three types of data: labels, numbers, and formulas. As soon as you begin typing in a cell entry, the mode indicator changes
from READY to either VALUE or LABEL.

LABELS

A label usually begins with a letter. A label may *not* begin with any character
that can be interpreted as a number, which includes 0 through 9, as well as the
plus, minus, decimal point, dollar sign, and parentheses symbols.

If you were to type in a local phone number of three digits, a hyphen, and four
more digits, Lotus 1-2-3 would assume that the data was numeric. Since the
hyphen also symbolizes a dash meaning subtraction, upon pressing ⏎, the
last four digits would be subtracted from the first three. When numeric characters like a phone number need to be treated as labels, you precede the entry
with a label prefix.

Label data is always preceded by a ***label prefix character*** instructing Lotus
1-2-3 where to place the data in a cell. If you do not enter a label prefix character while typing a label, Lotus 1-2-3 inserts the prefix to left-align the data, but
you can also position label data in a cell left-aligned, centered, or right-aligned.

The apostrophe (') label prefix is the default whenever the first character of a
cell's contents is a letter. Unless a label must start with something other than a
letter, or a label must be positioned to the right (right-aligned) or centered in a
field as opposed to beginning at the left edge of the cell, it is *not* necessary to
type in a label prefix.

The four label prefixes are shown below.

'	Apostrophe	Left-Aligns an entry to a cell as a label.
"	Quotation mark	Right-aligns an entry to a cell as a label.
^	Caret	Centers an entry to a cell as a label (located at the top of the IBM PC keyboard—press ⇧Shift-6).
\	Backslash	Repeats the designated label within the cell (not to be confused with the forward slash, /, used to activate the menu bar).

NUMBERS

A number entry contains actual numeric *values* and may involve subsequent calculations. A number must begin with one of the following characters:

0 1 2 3 4 5 6 7 8 9 . + – $ (

Punctuation, such as the comma, the dollar sign, and percent symbol, should not be entered with the numbers; for example, the number 1,024 should be entered as 1024. You can add numeric punctuation with Lotus 1-2-3's formatting options. Be sure that numeric entries do not contain spaces or more than one decimal point.

FORMULAS

Formulas perform mathematical operations and display the results in a cell. A formula must begin with one of the following characters:

0 1 2 3 4 5 6 7 8 9 . (@ # $ + –

Lotus 1-2-3 evaluates formulas from left to right, and follows standard order of precedence rules. These rules generally state that all exponential operations are completed first, followed by multiplication and division, then by addition and subtraction operations in the order they are encountered in the formula. If any part of the formula is enclosed in parentheses, that part is completed first. For example, if a formula contains instructions for both addition and multiplication, the multiplication takes place before the addition.

The operators listed next are in the required order for calculations to be performed.

( )   Parentheses (used for grouping)

^   Caret (indicates exponential operations)

*   Multiplication

/   Division

+   Addition

–   Subtraction

Formulas often include cell locations. For example, suppose that you want to add the contents of cells A1 and A2. The formula would have to begin with a numeric character and would have to be entered as +A1+A2.

The Gross Profit formula in the Monthly Income Statement model illustrates a formula preceded by a math operator. The second formula utilizes a Lotus 1-2-3 *function*, which automates numerous common calculations. Functions start with @ preceding the function name, followed by specified parameters enclosed within parentheses. @SUM(A1..A2) means to add the contents of the cells in range A1..A2. Generally, when you have four or more contiguous cells to reference in a formula, you write them as a range. Refer to the Lotus 1-2-3 manual for a complete description of functions.

BASIC EDITING PROCEDURES

You will probably spend as much time changing data that is already stored in a cell as you do entering new data. Four techniques for changing data are discussed below. Follow these procedures for editing data in Lotus 1-2-3.

➤ To change data while still typing the cell contents:

1. Use [Backspace] to remove the error(s).

2. Retype the entry.

➤ To change cell contents of short entries once [↵] has been pressed and the data is placed in a cell:

1. Position the pointer in the cell containing the error.

2. Retype the entry and press [↵].

➤ To change the cell contents of longer entries:

1. Press [F2] to enter EDIT mode. Notice that the mode indicator in the upper-right corner of the screen changes to EDIT.

2. Use the pointer movement keys to position the cursor in the cell. Insert and/or delete characters as needed.

3. Press [↵] to complete editing that cell. Refer to the table of special Edit keys in the "Keyboard" section of **Introduction to Lotus 1-2-3**.

➤ To delete the contents of any cell:

1. Position the cell pointer in the cell.

2. Press / to activate the Main menu.

3. Select **R**ange **E**rase.

4. Press [↵] to accept the range to erase as the current cell position shown in the Control Panel.

CHANGING COLUMN WIDTH

Initially the columns on a blank worksheet are nine characters wide. You can change the default setting to a width from 1 to 240. During the worksheet design phase, estimate the column widths you will need based on the maximum length of data to be entered. For example, if you plan to enter account titles in column A, decide if the longest label you might enter would be 15, 20, or 25 characters. You can always adjust your original estimate by narrowing or widening columns as you work.

One or more columns can be changed in a single operation depending on the command sequence you select. Select /**W**orksheet **C**olumn to access a menu of options that apply to individual columns.

```
A1:                                                              MENU
Set-Width  Reset-Width  Hide  Display  Column-Range
Specify width for current column
```

Select **S**et-Width to change the width of the column in which the cell pointer currently appears. Select **C**olumn-Range (Release 2.0 and higher) to change widths of a user-specified set of adjacent columns. The width you specify appears within square brackets in line 1 of the Control Panel whenever the cell pointer appears in a column set by either of these options. The other choices allow you to reset the column width to the default, to hide one or more columns from view or from printed output, and to restore hidden columns.

To select a primary column width for the worksheet as a whole, select /**W**orksheet **G**lobal **C**olumn-Width. The specification of a width in this manner does not override existing individual column width settings, nor does it prevent you from changing individual column widths later.

► To widen column A to 25 characters:

1. Access a blank worksheet screen in READY mode.

2. Position the cell pointer in column A.

3. Press /.

   Check that your screen resembles the one shown in the following figure.

```
A1:                                                              MENU
Worksheet  Range  Copy  Move  File  Print  Graph  Data  System  Add-In  Quit
Global  Insert  Delete  Column  Erase  Titles  Window  Status  Page  Learn
```

The highlighted bar in the Control Panel rests on the **W**orksheet option, but no selection from the Main menu has been made yet. The submenu in the third line shows the set of choices available if the **W**orksheet option is selected.

4. Press **W** or ⏎ and see the Control Panel as shown in the following figure.

```
A1:                                                              MENU
Global  Insert  Delete  Column  Erase  Titles  Window  Status  Page  Learn
Format  Label-Prefix  Column-Width  Recalculation  Protection  Default  Zero
```

5. Select **C**olumn.

6. Select **S**et-Width.

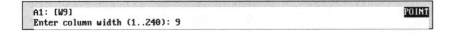
```
A1: [W9]                                                         POINT
Enter column width (1..240): 9
```

7. Type **25** at the "Enter column width:" prompt and press ⏎.

   Check that column A has been widened to 25 characters.

➤ To set a global column width of 12:

1. Select /**W**orksheet **G**lobal.

    Now that you are familiar with the sequential nature of making menu selections, more than one menu choice may appear in a single instruction. Complete each part of the instruction in order from left to right. In this case, press /, select the **W**orksheet option from line 2 of the Control Panel, and then select **G**lobal from the new menu that appears in line 2.

2. Select **C**olumn-Width.

3. Type **12** and press ⏎ at the "Enter global column width:" prompt.

ENTERING DATA

To enter data into a worksheet, position the cell pointer on the cell where the data is to be entered, type the data, and press ⏎ to transfer the characters into the cell.

ENTERING LABELS AND NUMBERS

➤ To enter a worksheet title:

1. Position the cell pointer in cell A1.

2. Type **SAMPLE COMPANY**

    The characters you type appear in the second line of the Control Panel. If you notice a mistake in the typed characters, repeatedly press [Backspace] until you remove the error and then continue typing.

3. Press ⏎.

You can also accept entry of cell A1's contents and automatically position the cell pointer in A2 for the next cell entry by pressing ⬇.

➤ To enter labels, type the data into the cells indicated (press ⏎ after typing each cell's contents):

1. At cell A2 type **Monthly Income Statement: 1992**

    The contents of cell A2 display in the worksheet across both cells A2 and B2. Even though Lotus 1-2-3 permits label data that is too wide for the cell it is stored in to be displayed into adjacent empty cells, the entire description is stored in memory as the content only of cell A2.

2. At cell A7 type **Sales**

3. At cell A8 type **Less Cost of Goods Sold**

4. At cell A10 type **Gross Profit**

5. At cell A11 type **Less Operating Expenses:**

6. At cell A12 type **Selling**

7. At cell A13 type **Administrative**

8. At cell A15 type **Total Expenses**

9. At cell A17 type **Net Income**

    Check that your screen matches the one shown in the following figure.

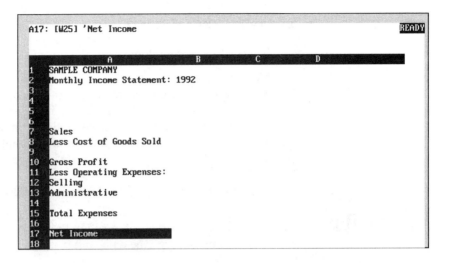

➤ **To enter the initial January numbers and the remaining labels for SAMPLE COMPANY:**

1. At cell B5 type **^JAN**

2. At cell B7 type **10000**

3. At cell B8 type **6200**

4. At cell B9 type **"- - - - - - - - - -** (quotation mark and 10 hyphens).

5. At cell B12 type **1200**

6. At cell B13 type **1800**

7. At cell B16 type **"- - - - - - - - - -** (quotation mark and 10 hyphens).

8. At cell B18 type **"= = = = = = = = = =** (quotation mark and 10 equals signs)

    Check your results with the following figure.

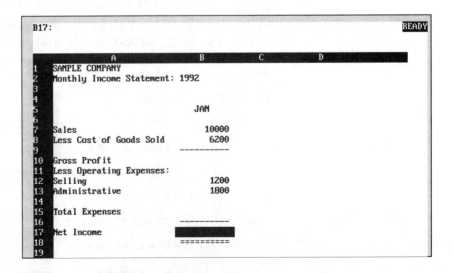

ENTERING FORMULAS

Always use formulas to produce calculated results in a worksheet, as opposed to typing the numeric answer into a cell. That way, if you change any number that has an impact on a formula, the formula's result automatically recalculates. You must begin a formula with a math symbol (such as the + sign).

➤ To enter the January formulas and check your results:

1. At cell B10 type **+B7−B8**

2. At cell B15 type **@SUM(B12..B13)**

   Typing **+B12+B13** produces the same results.

3. At cell B17 type **+B10−B15**

Compare your results with the following figure.

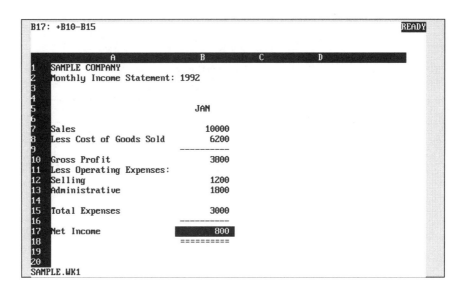

SPECIFYING NUMBER FORMATS

You can change the display of numeric data by executing a Format command for the worksheet as a whole or for any portion (range) of the worksheet. Changing the format that a cell uses to display its numeric contents can result in the cell's contents exceeding the column width, and you may need to alter the column width. For example, the number 1234.56 in the *Fixed format* with two decimal places is only seven characters long. However, if the cell format were changed to the *Currency format* with two decimal places, the same number would appear as $1,234.56, which is nine characters long.

If the displayed value in a cell exceeds the width of the column containing the cell, asterisks (********) appear. The computer's memory still contains the value out to 15 decimal places, but the value can't be displayed until the column is widened.

➤ **To set a global (entire worksheet) format of "comma" (comma to separate thousands, no dollar sign):**

1. Select /Worksheet Global Format.

2. Select , to specify the Comma format.

    Check that your screen matches the one shown in the following figure.

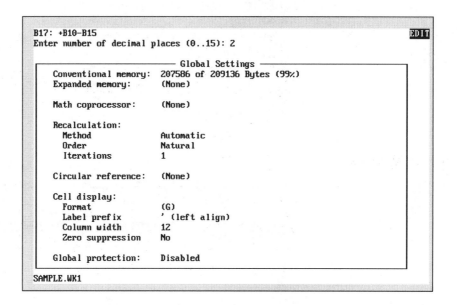

```
B17: +B10-B15                                                      EDIT
Enter number of decimal places (0..15): 2
                          ── Global Settings ──
       Conventional memory:  207586 of 209136 Bytes (99%)
       Expanded memory:      (None)

       Math coprocessor:     (None)

       Recalculation:
         Method              Automatic
         Order               Natural
         Iterations          1

       Circular reference:   (None)

       Cell display:
         Format              (G)
         Label prefix        ' (left align)
         Column width        12
         Zero suppression    No

       Global protection:    Disabled

SAMPLE.WK1
```

3. Press ↵ to accept the default setting of two decimal places when prompted to "Enter number of decimal places (0..15): 2."

➤ **To follow the accounting convention of having the first and last figures in columns preceded by a dollar sign:**

1. Select /Range Format Currency.

2. Press ↵ at the "Enter number of decimal places (0..15): 2" prompt.

3. Type **B7..G7** and press ↵ to accept the range to be formatted.

    All six columns are formatted in anticipation of entering six months of data.

4. Select /Range Format Currency.

5. Press ↵ at the "Enter number of decimal places (0..15): 2" prompt.

6. Type **B17..G17** and press ↵ to accept the range to be formatted.

    Check that your screen matches the one shown in the following figure.

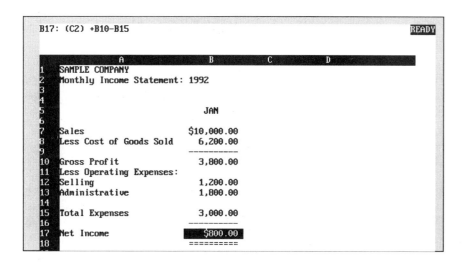

SAVING THE WORKSHEET

Lotus 1-2-3 does not provide an automatic **S**ave feature. In the event of a power interruption, any changes made to the worksheet since you last saved it will not be saved to disk.

After initiating a **S**ave operation, you are prompted to enter a file name. The default drive and path, often called the current directory, appear in the Control Panel, as shown in the next figure.

The directory path illustrates storing data files in the R2DATA subdirectory of the 123R2 directory on drive C:. The path you see depends on how Lotus 1-2-3 was installed on your system. If the displayed path is correct for saving the current worksheet, add a file name that can include up to eight characters. Lotus 1-2-3 provides the extension (.WKE, educational release; .WKS, version 1A; .WK1, Releases 2.0, 2.01, 2.2, and 2.3; .WK3, Releases 3.0 and 3.1).

To specify a different path only for the current **S**ave operation, press Esc enough times to blank out unwanted portions of the displayed path, and then type the desired alternative. Project 3 contains instructions for changing the displayed path for the duration of your work in Lotus 1-2-3.

If the file name you type already exists, a menu appears with the three options **C**ancel, **R**eplace, and **B**ackup (early versions of Lotus 1-2-3 do not include **B**ackup). If you do not want the current worksheet to overwrite the file on disk, select **C**ancel, then repeat the **S**ave process specifying a different file name. Choose **R**eplace to update the file on disk.

The **B**ackup option changes the extension of the file on disk to .BAK and saves the current worksheet. For example, if you specified the name SAMPLE and selected **B**ackup, two files named SAMPLE.WK1 and SAMPLE.BAK would be stored on disk. With this option you can save both the current version and the most recent prior version.

➤ To save the initial worksheet model:

1. Select /File Save.

2. Check that the correct path appears in the Control Panel, such as A:, B:, or C:\123\123DATA. If incorrect, press [Esc] enough times to clear the unwanted portion, and then type the correct drive and path for your system.

3. Type **SAMPLE** and press [↵].

PRINTING THE WORKSHEET

Most users need hard copies of worksheets as well as the ability to retrieve files to screen display. Use the **Print** command to produce hard copy of worksheets or databases. Printing graphs requires a special utility program, called PrintGraph, in all releases of Lotus 1-2-3 except Release 3.0.

Select /**Print P**rinter when you have a printer on-line. Select /**Print F**ile FILE-NAME when you want to print your output into a disk file and print it to paper later using the DOS TYPE command or your word processor. Either way, you must then specify a print range, select from options if desired, and execute the command.

Before printing your worksheet, save your work.

➤ To access the main printer menu:

1. Select /**P**rint.

   Check that the print output options appear in the Control Panel as shown in the following figure.

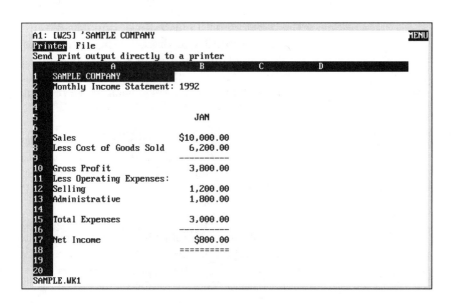

```
A1: [W25] 'SAMPLE COMPANY                                              MENU
Printer  File
Send print output directly to a printer
            A                    B            C            D
1   SAMPLE COMPANY
2   Monthly Income Statement: 1992
3
4
5                               JAN
6
7   Sales                  $10,000.00
8   Less Cost of Goods Sold  6,200.00
9                           ----------
10  Gross Profit             3,800.00
11  Less Operating Expenses:
12  Selling                  1,200.00
13  Administrative           1,800.00
14
15  Total Expenses           3,000.00
16                          ----------
17  Net Income                $800.00
18                          ==========
19
20
SAMPLE.WK1
```

2. Select **P**rinter.

   Check that the main printer menu shown in the following figure appears on your screen.

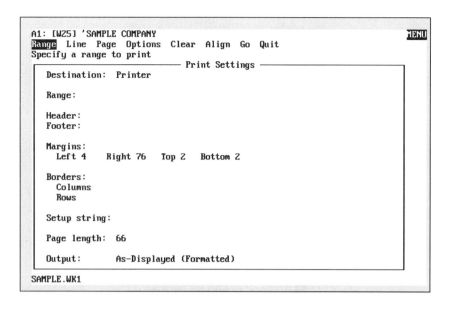

```
A1: [W25] 'SAMPLE COMPANY                                    MENU
Range  Line  Page  Options  Clear  Align  Go  Quit
Specify a range to print
┌───────────────────────── Print Settings ─────────────────────────┐
│  Destination:  Printer                                            │
│                                                                   │
│  Range:                                                           │
│                                                                   │
│  Header:                                                          │
│  Footer:                                                          │
│                                                                   │
│  Margins:                                                         │
│    Left 4      Right 76    Top 2    Bottom 2                       │
│                                                                   │
│  Borders:                                                         │
│    Columns                                                        │
│    Rows                                                           │
│                                                                   │
│  Setup string:                                                    │
│                                                                   │
│  Page length:  66                                                 │
│                                                                   │
│  Output:        As-Displayed (Formatted)                          │
└───────────────────────────────────────────────────────────────────┘
SAMPLE.WK1
```

➤ **To set the print range and print the first month's data:**

1. Select **R**ange.

    You can print any range of data from a single cell to the entire worksheet. To specify the range to be printed, type or point to the cell range. When you mark a print range, it remains set until you enter a new range. If you want to use these printer settings the next time you retrieve the worksheet, be sure to save the worksheet before exiting the program.

2. Type **A1..B18** and press ⏎ at the "Enter print range" prompt.

    Check that your printer is turned on and that paper is properly aligned at the top of a blank page.

3. Select **A**lign to set Lotus 1-2-3's internal line counter to line 1.

4. Select **G**o to begin printing.

    Check that you printed the specified data range shown in the following figure.

```
SAMPLE COMPANY
 Monthly Income Statement: 1992


                                        JAN

Sales                                $10,000.00
Less Cost of Goods Sold                6,200.00
                                     -----------
Gross Profitve                         3,800.00
Less Operating Expenses:
Selling                                1,200.00
Administrative                         1,800.00

Total Expenses                         3,000.00
                                     -----------
Net Income                        $      800.00
                                     ===========
```

5. Select **Page** to feed paper.

6. Select **Quit** to exit the Printer menu and restore READY mode.

ERASING THE CURRENT WORKSHEET

When you are finished with the current worksheet, you can take one of three actions: create a new worksheet, retrieve another worksheet, or exit the program. Only the first activity requires that you erase the current worksheet. Before you execute the **Erase** command, be sure to save any changes if you wish to keep the data stored on disk.

➤ To erase the current worksheet:

1. Select **/W**orksheet Erase.

2. Select **Yes**.

You have now completed this project. You may either go on to the Study Questions and Review Exercises and the next topic, or end your Lotus 1-2-3 session by selecting **/Q**uit.

SUMMARY

- Worksheet cells may contain three types of data: labels, numbers, and formulas. Plan the layout of the worksheet before you begin to enter data.

- Cell entries that are non-numeric are called labels. A label usually begins with a letter and can be left-aligned, centered, or right-aligned in a cell by specifying a label prefix.

- A number entry contains actual numeric values displayed right-aligned and may involve subsequent calculations. Punctuation such as the comma and symbols such as the $ or % should not be entered with the numbers.

- Formulas perform math operations and display the results in a right-aligned location in a cell. A formula must begin with one of the following characters: 0 1 2 3 4 5 6 7 8 9 . (@ # $ + -

- The four label prefixes are ' (left-align), " (right-align), ^ (center), and \ (repeat cell contents).

- Columns in the worksheet initially display with a nine-character width. You can set a new width from 1 to 240 (1 to 72 in Lotus 1-2-3 version 1A) for the worksheet as a whole or for individual columns.

- Format commands change the display of numeric data for the worksheet as a whole or for any portion (range) of the worksheet.

- You provide up to eight characters for a file name when you save a worksheet. Lotus 1-2-3 provides three-character extensions that begin with "WK" and end with a character associated with each release.

- You use the **Print** command to produce hard copy of worksheets or databases. You can sent output to a printer or to a disk file.

- To access a blank worksheet after you have been working in Lotus 1-2-3, you erase the current worksheet.

KEY TERMS

Currency format	function	long label
Fixed format	label	number
formula	label prefix character	value

STUDY QUESTIONS

TRUE/FALSE

1. Cell contents that begin with a numeric character (0 to 9) or the @ # $. (+ - symbols are called values. **T** F

2. A formula can contain cell references, functions, and numbers. **T** F

3. In a formula, addition and subtraction are always performed before multiplication and division. T **F**

4. Labels are always preceded by a label prefix that determines the position of the label within a cell. T **F**

5. A caret (^) typed in front of a cell's contents causes the contents to be treated as a label, even if the contents begin with a number from 0 to 9. T **F**

6. If a label is too long to fit in a cell, you must widen the cell in order to see the entire label. T **F**

7. The portion of a value that is too large to be displayed in a cell will display in the adjacent cell if that cell is empty. **T** F

8. A worksheet is saved each time it is recalculated. T **F**

9. Before a worksheet can be printed, the range of cells to be printed must be specified. **T** F

10. Changing the format of a cell can cause the value in the cell to become too large to be displayed. **T** F

FILL IN THE BLANKS

1. Labels are always preceded by a label _____'_____.

2. A repeating label is preceded by the __________ character.

3. Before a worksheet can be printed, a __Range__ of cells must be specified.

4. Each time a cell containing a formula changes, the worksheet is __update__.

5. To save a worksheet, use the / __File__ Save option.

6. When saving a worksheet, if a file of the same name is already on disk, you are prompted to cancel, __Save__, or back up.

7. A label that is too long to fit in a cell will be displayed in the adjacent cell if that cell is __Empty__.

8. To right-justify the label contents of a cell, precede the contents with a _____"_____ character.

9. When a value is too large to be displayed in a cell, __* * *__ replace the value in the cell display.

10. To edit a cell, position the cell pointer on the cell and press __F2__.

SHORT ANSWER

1. Discuss the purpose of label prefix characters.

2. Briefly describe the purpose of a formula.

3. Describe why changing the format of a cell might cause the cell display to change to all asterisks.

4. Describe how a number—for example, the year 1992—can be centered in a cell as a heading.

5. Discuss how Lotus 1-2-3 displays long labels.

REVIEW EXERCISES

You are likely to own many items classified as personal property, including clothes, books, stereo, tape or CD collection, and a personal computer system. For insurance purposes, it is a good idea to keep a record of the original cost of such items. To analyze whether you have sufficient insurance coverage, you might also calculate the estimated replacement costs.

You can practice the concepts presented in Project 1 by completing the following tasks to create, save, and print a Personal Property worksheet. If necessary, review the material presented in the project in order to complete the tasks.

1. Access a blank worksheet and enter the worksheet title (cell A1), documentation (cell A2), and column headings shown in the following figure. The width of column A has been changed to 20 in the figure, but you should specify the column widths you think are appropriate for your data.

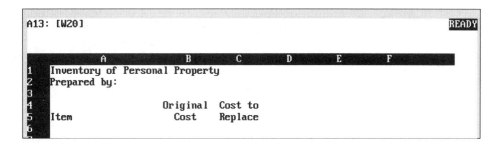

```
A13: [W20]                                                    READY

                   A            B        C        D        E        F
1   Inventory of Personal Property
2   Prepared by:
3
4                           Original  Cost to
5   Item                       Cost   Replace
6
```

2.   Beginning in row 6, enter data about your personal property. For example, you might enter Clothes in cell A6, Stereo in cell A7, and so on. Estimate and enter the original and replacement costs, rounded to whole dollars. (For example, if an item cost $123.78, enter 124.)

3.   Alter the display of all numeric data to the Comma format, zero decimal places.

4.   Enter separator lines in columns B and C immediately below the row containing the last personal property item.

5.   In the row below the separator lines, enter formulas in columns B and C to total the original costs and replacement costs. Use the @SUM function in the formulas. For example, if your last original cost was entered in row 15, enter the formula @SUM(B6..B15).

6.   Alter the numeric display of the first and last amounts in columns B and C to the Currency format, zero decimal places.

7.   Save the worksheet under the file name PERSPROP.

8.   After printing the worksheet, access a blank worksheet.

 # COMPETENCY TESTING

- Review the Topic Objectives to ensure you have mastered all skills listed.

- Ask your Class Assistant to check off:

  - Your completed Project work (the printed worksheet file SAMPLE).

  - Your completed True/False and Fill in the Blanks exercises.

  - Your completed Review Exercises (the printout of PERSPROP and your TDL).

- Ask your Class Assistant to see the **Creating a Worksheet**:

  - **Project Sample Sheet** to compare your work against the sample.

  - **True/False and Fill in the Blanks Correct Answer Sheet** to compare your answers against the correct ones.

  - **Review Exercises Sample Answer Sheet** to compare your work against it.

MODIFYING AND DOCUMENTING A WORKSHEET

TOPIC OBJECTIVES
· · · · · · · · · · · ·

After completing this topic you should be able to:

- Retrieve a worksheet.

- Use prefix characters to align labels within a range of cells.

- Copy or move cell contents.

- Format a range containing formulas as text.

- Use relative and absolute cell addressing.

- Switch between automatic and manual recalculation.

- View two portions of a worksheet.

  - Freeze titles.

  - Use worksheet window.

- Name cell ranges.

- Use range name in formulas.

- Edit formulas.

- Insert and delete columns or rows.

- Edit or erase cell contents.

- Use and/or identify Lotus 1-2-3's set of built-in @functions (@SUM, @DATE, @NOW, @COUNT, @ROUND, @INT, @AVG, @MIN, @MAX, @PMT).

- Use @function to date stamp a worksheet (@NOW).

- Print worksheet contents cell by cell (cell contents and cell attributes).

- Use "what if" analysis (*Note*: Covered in Computer Tutorial *only*).

COMPUTER TUTORIAL
· · · · · · · · · · · ·

- From the **Novice** section, work through:

  C Create a worksheet (review "freeze labels", if necessary; done last topic)

  G Perform calculations (second half of option G, as follows):

    - Copy a formula from one cell to a range of cells

    - Learn about relative and absolute cell addressing

    - Edit the contents of a cell

H   Use logical functions

I   Use a scoreboard

J   Split a worksheet into two windows

 PRACTICE EXERCISES

- Read and complete all **Project 2 work** outlined on pages 37 to 59:

  - Take special note of the **Key Terms** and **Summary** sections.

  - Be sure to save the worksheet **SAMPLE**, as indicated on page 52. (Note that saving SAMPLE here overwrites the copy of SAMPLE already on disk from the **Creating a Worksheet** topic: therefore, be sure you have had the first version checked off in the Creating a Worksheet topic before you overwrite it.)

  - Be sure to keep the cell contents printout (pages 57 and 58).

- After finishing all Project work on pages 37 to 59, print a **directory listing** in the same manner as you usually create your TDL.

- Do **True/False** exercises on pages 59 and 60.

- Do **Fill in the Blanks** exercises on pages 60.

- Do all **Review Exercises** on page 61, making sure to save **PERSPROP** and do the two printouts indicated. (Note that saving PERSPROP here overwrites the copy of PERSPROP already on disk from the **Creating a Worksheet** topic: therefore, be sure you have had the first version checked off in the Creating a Worksheet topic before you overwrite it here.)

- Do the required **Topic Directory Listing (TDL)**. If you've forgotten, see **Introduction to Lotus 1-2-3**: Practice Exercises section for an explanation.

NOTE

- Spreadsheets' most powerful capacity is the facility for "what-if" analysis. Since any number of formulas in worksheet cells can be linked, or related, to each other, it is possible to ask "what if I change one piece of data in one cell ... what effect will that have on results in related cells?"

  Because "what-if" analysis is both basic and central to spreadsheets, you can expect to be asked to demonstrate the ability to perform it on the module competency test. "What-if" analysis is covered in detail in the computer tutorial for this topic, but here is another example for you to use to build and practice your skills.

Assume that you are selling memberships to a health club. The club allows you to sell these memberships at either the "full" price of $120 or the "discounted" ("special") price of $80. You're allowed to decide how many you want to sell at which price, but you have to give the health club $100 for each membership you sell, regardless of which price you charged the new member. You know that discounting prices is a good way to stimulate market interest, but it's also clear that if you sold all memberships at the discounted price of $80, you'd owe the club money out of your own pocket, since they expect $100 from you for each one sold. That kind of math is obvious! A spreadsheet, however, allows you to easily work out the less clear solutions to problems like "how many memberships would I have to sell at the full price to make $600 for myself?"

An approximation of the spreadsheet you'll need is shown below:

	A	B	C	D	E	F
1			Num	Price		Amount
2	SALES					
3		Regular		120		
4		Discount		80		
5		Total				
6						
7	EXPENSES					
8		Owe club	50	100		
9						
10	INCOME					

Enter all of the labels (all are left-aligned, the default, except for those in Row 1, which are right-aligned), then put in the values you know: enter the full price for memberships in D3 (120), the discounted price in D4 (80), and the price you'll have to pay the club in D8 (100). Assume that you'll be selling fifty (50) memberships in total, and enter that value in C8. Later, you're going to be putting a value representing the number of memberships you sell at the full price in C3, so leave that cell empty for now. You can, however, put something in C4: enter the formula 50-C3. That will calculate the number you sell at the discounted price whenever a value is entered in C3. You need to put a formula in F3 to calculate the amount you'll collect when you sell memberships at the regular price. This formula will be number sold times price, or +C3*D3. Figure out the similar formula to calculate the amount you'll collect when you sell memberships at the discounted price, and put that formula in F4 (Hint: /Copy might be helpful here). Now, enter something in F5 to add up the total amount you'll collect (Hint: @SUM might be helpful). Enter another formula in F8 similar to those in F3 and F4 to show the amount you'll have to give to the club (it will be number sold times the $100 price you have to pay the club). Finally, enter a formula in F10 to show you your net income. This is simply the money you take in (calculated in F5) less the money you have to give to the club (in F8).

Now you're ready to do "what-if" analysis. Your task will be to decide upon a balance of sales to guarantee yourself $600 net income. In other words, you'll be asking, for example, "what if I sold twenty-five memberships at the full price (and, therefore, twenty-five at the discounted price) ... would that give me $600?" Try it! Enter 25 in C3 and watch what happens to your net income in F10 ... oops! ... that didn't work! Continue trying different values in C3 until you find the one that gives you your $600.

If you have difficulty, your Class Assistant has the solution. Try to work it out on your own, though, and if you have to peek, then change some of the numbers to make a new problem, and play with the spreadsheet until you feel you fully understand "what-if" analysis.

- The concept of naming a range of worksheet cells sometimes gives new users difficulties, and so the explanation found in the section "Naming Cell Ranges" on pages 49 to 51 is very important.

  Often we name ranges simply to make working with the spreadsheet easier. (The example that follows is new; it does *not* refer back to the health club spreadsheet above.)

  Suppose you put the total value of a salesperson's sales in A1, and her commission rate (5% of total sales, for example) in B1. You might then put her salary in C1. To calculate her salary you would enter the following formula in C1:   +A1*B1.

  Now suppose you had used range names. You could name A1, TOTSALES, and name B1, COMRATE. Now the formula in C1 to calculate salary would be +TOTSALES*COMRATE, which may make more sense to you, and be more obvious, than +A1*B1.

  The above example is important for two reasons. First, it shows that naming cells may make your work more intuitive. Second, it demonstrates that you can perform mathematical operations on range names in the same ways as you do with respect to cell references. In other words, you can multiply TOTSALES by COMRATE in the same way as you can multiply A1 by B1. This holds for all operations.

PROJECT 2: MODIFYING AND DOCUMENTING A WORKSHEET

RETRIEVING A WORKSHEET

You will want to retrieve any worksheet stored on disk to review or revise its contents, include the data in a graph, or output the data to a printer. Just as you specified a disk drive\directory\path and file name to save a file, you must specify the same information when you retrieve a file stored on disk.

After initiating a **Retrieve** operation, you are prompted to enter a file name as shown in the following figure.

The default drive and path (also called the current directory) appear in line 2 of the Control Panel. The names of files stored in the current directory are displayed on line 3.

In the figure, the directory path illustrates retrieving data files from the R2DATA subdirectory of the 123R2 directory on drive C:. The path you see depends on how Lotus 1-2-3 was installed on your system. If the displayed path is correct for retrieving the current worksheet, type the desired file name, or use arrow keys to highlight the file name in line 3 and press ⏎.

To specify a different path only for the current **Retrieve** operation, press [Esc] enough times to blank out unwanted portions of the displayed path, then type the desired alternative. Project 3 contains instructions for changing the displayed path for the duration of your work in Lotus 1-2-3.

➤ **To retrieve the worksheet SAMPLE:**

1.   Select **/File Retrieve**.

2.   Check that the correct path appears in the Control Panel, such as A:, B:, or C:\123\123DATA. If incorrect, press [Esc] enough times to clear the unwanted portion, and then type the correct disk drive and path for your system.

3.   Type **SAMPLE** or highlight SAMPLE.WK1 in line 3 of the Control Panel, and press ⏎.

CELL RANGES

A *range* in Lotus 1-2-3 is a rectangle of cells within the worksheet, designated by referring to any two opposing corners. Normally, a range is referred to by its upper-left and lower-right cells. For example, a range of cells formed from the first two rows and first three columns of a worksheet would be designated as A1..C2. Range coordinates may be typed in uppercase or lowercase (letters), with two periods between each cell. You can type only one period and let Lotus 1-2-3 insert the second period.

The following figures illustrate examples of valid ranges.

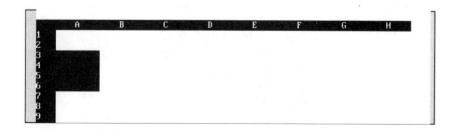

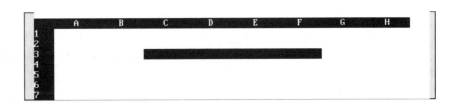

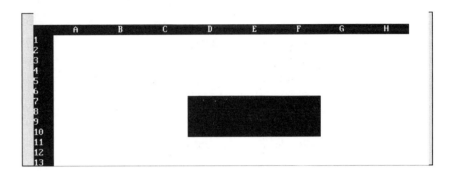

ALIGNING ENTRIES WITHIN A RANGE OF CELLS

If you enter label data without a label prefix (' to left-align, ^ to center, or " to right-align), the label appears left-aligned in the cell. If you have a series of labels to center or right-align in adjacent cells, you will find it easier to type the entries without label prefixes and specify alignment in a single command. Lotus 1-2-3 provides a **R**ange **L**abel command to align labels in a range of cells.

➤ **To enter additional column headings in the SAMPLE worksheet:**

1. Access the SAMPLE worksheet in READY mode.

2. At cell C5 type **FEB**

3. At cell D5 type **MAR**

4. At cell E5 type **APR**

5. At cell F5 type **MAY**

6. At cell G5 type **JUN**

➤ **To center the new column headings:**

1. Position the cell pointer in cell C5.

2. Select **/R**ange **L**abel.

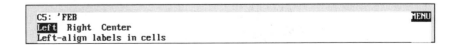

3. Select **C**enter.

4. Press ➡ a sufficient number of times to highlight the range C5..G5 and press ↵.

MOVING CELL CONTENTS

Both the Move and the Copy operations require specification of a range to move or copy FROM, followed by a range to move or copy TO. The range from which the data is being moved or copied is referred to as the *source* range. The range that is to receive the data is referred to as the *target* range.

Use the Move command to transfer a range of cells from one location on a worksheet to another. If you need to change the layout of your worksheet, Move lets you rearrange the data without disturbing the relations between the cells you have already defined. The Move command automatically adjusts all formulas in the worksheet to account for the changes made by transferring the data.

Caution: If you move a range of cells to an area that already contains data, the moved data will automatically overwrite the previous data. Make sure the entire target range of cells is empty, or that you intend to replace the previous data stored there.

➤ **To move the subtitle of your SAMPLE COMPANY income statement:**

1. Position the cell pointer in cell A2.

2. Select /Move.

   Check that the source range is A2..A2.

3. Press ⏎ to accept A2 as the range to move data FROM.

4. Use the arrow keys to move the cell pointer to specify B1 as the target for A2.

5. Press ⏎ to complete the move.

   Check that the data from A2 "Monthly Income Statement: 1992" has been moved to B1.

For the purpose of this exercise, let's assume that this new location for the worksheet subtitle does not look as pleasing as the original display. Using the Move command, transfer the subtitle back to its original location at A2.

➤ **To restore the subtitle to its original location:**

1. Position the cell pointer in cell B1.

2. Select /Move.

   Check that the source range is B1..B1.

3. Press ⏎ to accept B1 as the range to move data FROM.

4. Use the arrow keys to move the cell pointer to the target at A2.

5. Press ⏎ to complete the move.

   Check that the subtitle now appears in cell A2.

COPYING LABELS AND NUMBERS

Copying a range that includes only labels or numbers duplicates the specified range and transfers an exact copy of those cells to a specified location.

To practice using the **Copy** command, expand the initial Income Statement model to include a separator line for the range C9..G9.

➤ **To use the Copy command to duplicate the contents of cell B9 into the range C9..G9:**

1. Position the cell pointer in cell B9.

2. Select **/C**opy.

   Check that the source range (range to copy FROM) is B9..B9.

3. Press ⏎ to accept B9 as the source range for the **Copy** operation.

4. Press → to position the cell pointer in C9.

5. Press **.** (period) to *anchor* the upper-left corner of the range to copy TO (the Control Panel should display the message "Enter range to copy TO: C9").

6. Press → four times to expand the highlighted target range to C9..G9.

   Check that your screen matches the one shown in the following figure.

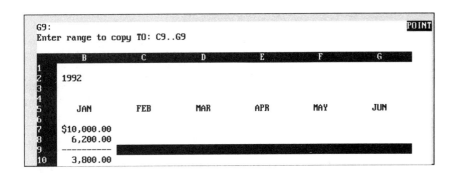

7. Press ⏎ to accept C9..G9 as the target range, and complete the **Copy** operation.

   Check that your results match those in the following figure.

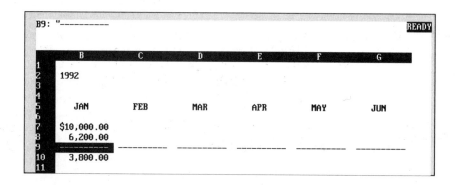

ADDRESSING

When you copy labels and numbers, Lotus 1-2-3 produces an exact copy of the source range in the target range. However, when you copy formulas that include cell addresses, the results vary depending on whether you specify relative, absolute, or mixed addressing in the formula(s) to be copied.

In a *relative address*, the highlighted cell is not a permanent address of a particular cell—in the example in the figure, D4—but a set of directions starting from another cell.

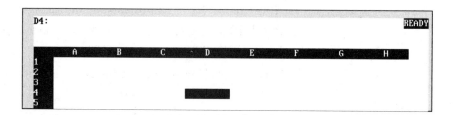

For example, if a formula in A1 referred to the highlighted cell, the formula would identify the highlighted cell as "three columns right and three rows down from this one." If the same formula were typed in G8, it would identify the highlighted cell as "three columns left and four rows up from this one." Unless you specify otherwise, cell addresses are relative.

An *absolute address* is a permanent reference to a specific cell. The absolute address of the same highlighted cell is D4, regardless of whatever cell you are referring to it.

A *mixed address* is one that is part relative and part absolute (either the column letter or the row number remains constant).

For example, if a formula in A1 referred to the address $D4, it would identify $D4 as "the cell in column D, three rows down." If the same formula was in cell G8, it would identify $D4 as "the cell in column D, four rows up."

The concepts of relative, absolute, and mixed addresses will become clearer as you use different addressing techniques to copy formulas.

COPYING FORMULAS

For every month in the worksheet being developed, the formula in row 17 (Net Income) is derived by subtracting Total Expenses (row 15) from Gross Profit (row 10). Formulas that repeatedly reference the same positions are first entered to one cell, then copied to an appropriate range of cells.

For example, consider the following formulas to calculate Gross Profit from January through June:

At B10 +B7–B8   (January Gross Profit)

At C10 +C7–C8   (February Gross Profit)

.

.

.

At G10 +G7–G8   (June Gross Profit)

The formula in cell B10 references cells in column B, the formula in cell C10 references cells in column C, and so on. The calculation is Sales minus Cost of Goods Sold, but the specific values that are used shift by columns. Unless notified otherwise, Lotus 1-2-3 assumes that formulas copied to a range of cells follow this relative-addressing scheme.

In the next example, you will copy the formula already in cell B10 to monthly columns C through G. "0.00" displays in any row 10 cell that lacks data in rows 7 and 8 above it. Study the results by changing the format to text, and then restore the global Comma (,) format.

If formulas include cells without a special *$ symbol,* those cells adjust to new column and row designations if they are moved or copied. That is, the cells indicated stay relative to position on the worksheet.

➤ **To copy the Gross Profit formula in cell B10:**

1.   Select **/C**opy.

2.   Type **B10** and press ⏎ to specify the range to copy FROM.

3.   Type **C10..G10** and press ⏎ to specify the range to copy TO.

     Check that your screen matches the one shown in the following figure.

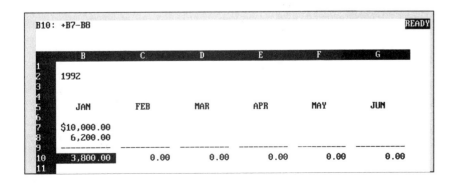

➤ **To view the Gross Profit formulas using the Text format and then reset the format:**

1. Select /**R**ange Format **T**ext.

2. Type **B10..G10** and press ↵ when prompted for the range to format.

    Check that your screen matches the one shown in the following figure.

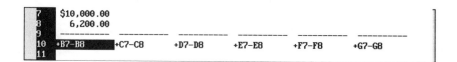

3. Select /**R**ange Format **R**eset.

4. Type **B10..G10** and press ↵ when prompted for the range to format.

Complete the initial framework for the January through June Income Statement data by copying two additional separator lines and the remaining formulas (Total Expenses and Net Income).

➤ **To copy separator lines and formulas from the January column of the Income Statement into the February through June columns:**

1. Position the cell pointer in cell B15.

2. Select /**C**opy.

3. Press ↓ three times to highlight the range B15..B18.

    Check your results against those in the following figure.

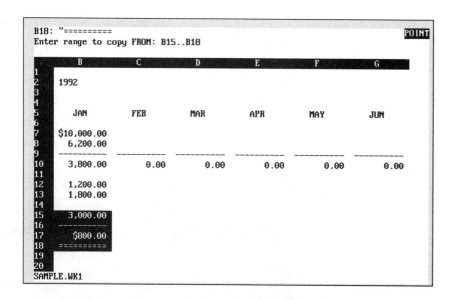

4. Press ↵ to specify the range to copy FROM.

5. Type **C15..G15** and press ↵ to specify the range to copy TO.

Check that the additional lines and formulas are in place (evidenced by the new $0.00 entries exhibited), as shown in the following figure. Separator lines appear in rows 16 and 18. Zeros display in rows 15 and 17, indicating that formulas are in place even though the actual Sales and Expense figures have not been entered yet. It is a common practice among developers of worksheets to set up a model for an entire time period.

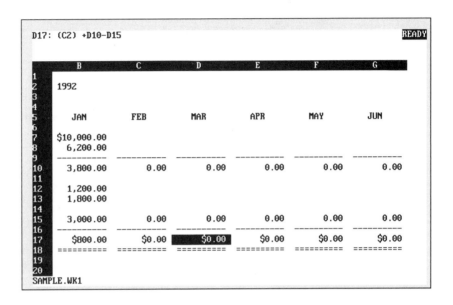

Position the cell pointer in several cells in rows 15 and 17 to verify that the formulas have copied correctly. Make any necessary corrections.

➤ **To save the expanded worksheet model:**

1. Select /**F**ile **S**ave.

2. Press ⏎ to accept the current name SAMPLE.

3. Select **R**eplace to update the file on disk.

SWITCHING TO MANUAL RECALCULATION

Each time you enter data into a cell, the worksheet is *recalculated*. As the size of your worksheet increases, the recalculation time becomes perceptibly longer. By default, Lotus 1-2-3 is set to recalculate automatically each time a cell changes. When entering data, you may find the recalculation time annoying if you can type faster than Lotus 1-2-3 can recalculate. You can temporarily switch to manual recalculation while you enter or edit the data, then press the CALC function key F9 to recompute the worksheet all at once when you are done.

Manual recalculation stays in effect until you issue the command to return to the automatic setting. The indicator CALC appears in the lower-right corner of the screen every time you make a worksheet change that has an impact on a formula while in Manual mode. CALC acts as a message to warn you that the worksheet is in Manual mode, and that you should press F9 to recompute the whole worksheet.

After setting recalculation to Manual, complete data entry (Sales, Cost of Goods Sold, Selling Expense, Administrative Expense) for the five additional months. Press F9 to recompute the worksheet and restore recalculation to Automatic.

► **To set recalculation to Manual mode:**

1.   Select **/W**orksheet **G**lobal **R**ecalculation **M**anual.

► **To enter data in cell C7:**

1.   Position the cell pointer in cell C7.

2.   Type **11000** and press ↵.

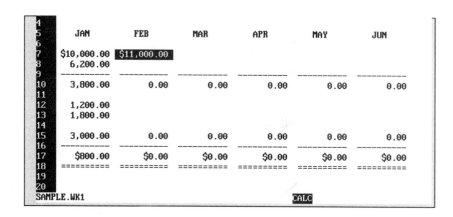

No formula in column C recalculates in spite of the addition of new data in cell C7 that has an impact on both the Gross Profit and Net Income formulas. The CALC message to warn you that the worksheet is not numerically correct stays in the lower-right corner of the screen until you press F9. *Do not press* F9 *yet*.

► **To enter the rest of the data:**

1.   At cell D7 type **12000**

2.   At cell E7 type **18000**

3.   At cell F7 type **15000**

4.   At cell G7 type **13000**

5.   At cell C8 type **6820**

6.   At cell D8 type **6600**

7.   At cell E8 type **10800**

8.   At cell F8 type **9000**

9.   At cell G8 type **8800**

10.   At cell C12 type **1320**

11. At cell D12 type **1500**

12. At cell E12 type **2300**

13. At cell F12 type **1800**

14. At cell G12 type **1500**

15. At cell C13 type **1980**

16. At cell D13 type **2500**

17. At cell E13 type **3100**

18. At cell F13 type **2700**

19. At cell G13 type **2300**

Compare your results with the worksheet shown in the following figure.

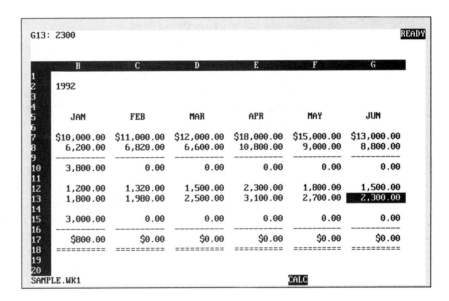

➤ **To recalculate the worksheet while in Manual mode:**

1. Press F9.

Compare your results with the worksheet shown in the following figure.

➤ **To restore Automatic recalculation and save the worksheet:**

1. Select /Worksheet Global Recalculation Automatic.

2. Select /File Save.

3. Press ⏎ to accept SAMPLE as the file name.

4. Select Replace.

VIEWING TWO PORTIONS OF A WORKSHEET

Worksheet data usually occupies more space than one screen can display. Lotus 1-2-3 provides two methods to view separate portions of a worksheet on a single screen. Both methods are initiated by selecting /Worksheet to access the menu shown in the following figure.

```
B22:                                                                    MENU
Global   Insert   Delete   Column   Erase   Titles   Window   Status   Page   Learn
Set horizontal or vertical titles
```

Select Titles to freeze the worksheet display at the left of (vertical), or above (horizontal), the current cell pointer position. This feature is most often used to keep the first few row and/or column headings on the screen at all times when the worksheet greatly exceeds the display area of one screen.

Select Window to split the screen into two parts to the left of, or above, the current cell pointer position. Press F6 to shift the cell pointer from one window to the other. Using cell pointer movement keys, you can position any section of a worksheet in either window. Unless you specify otherwise, the display in one window is synchronized to the display in the other window. For example, row 8 in the left half of a vertical window lines up with row 8 in the right half. If you want to see row 8 at the top of the screen in the left window and row 55 at the top of the screen in the right window, you would have to select the UN-SYNC option from the Window menu.

➤ **To freeze the titles and the monthly headings:**

1. Position the cell pointer in any cell in row 6, such as A6.

2. Select /Worksheet Titles Horizontal.

3. Press ⬇ until the cell pointer is in A23.

   Rows 6 through 8 should have scrolled off the screen; rows 1 through 5 remain. You will clear the title setting in a subsequent exercise.

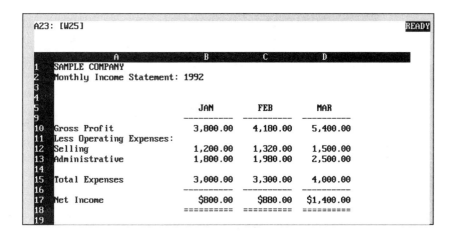

> To add Earnings per Share data (to be used in the next two exercises):

1. At cell A20 type **Earnings per Share**

2. At cell A23 type **Common Shares Outstanding**

3. At cell B23 type **1000**

4. Select **/R**ange **F**ormat **,**

5. Type **0** and press ⏎ at the "Enter number of decimal places:" prompt.

6. Type **B23** and press ⏎ at the "Enter range to format:" prompt.

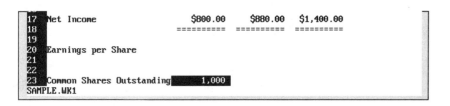

NAMING CELL RANGES

Certain cells are likely to be referenced often in formulas, such as Sales or Net Income amounts in the SAMPLE worksheet. Lotus 1-2-3 provides a feature to name a range and thereafter use the name in command sequences instead of having to remember the range's cell coordinates.

Press F3 to see a list of named ranges whenever POINT mode is active. The list initially appears in line 3 of the Control Panel. If you have a lot of range names defined, press F3 again for a full screen display of all range names. To select from either display, highlight your choice and press ⏎. You can, of course, type the desired range name in a formula or in response to a screen prompt for a range.

There are a few rules for selecting the name for a range. The name must not exceed 15 characters in length and should not contain spaces, numerals, or special characters.

➤ **To name the range of cells containing the January Net Income (B17) and the number of Common Shares Outstanding (B23) for subsequent use in a formula:**

1.   Select **/R**ange **N**ame **C**reate.

2.   Type **INCOME** and press ⏎ at the "Enter name:" prompt.

3.   Type **B17** and press ⏎ at the "Enter range:" prompt.

     The READY mode reappears. No change is apparent on the screen, but hereafter cell B17 may be referenced by using the word INCOME instead of the location B17.

4.   Select **/R**ange **N**ame **C**reate.

5.   Type **SHARES** and press ⏎ at the "Enter name:" prompt.

6.   Type **B23** and press ⏎ at the "Enter range:" prompt.

➤ **To enter a formula for January Earnings per Share that uses previously defined range names instead of cell references:**

1.   At cell B20 type **(INCOME)/SHARES**

     Check that your screen matches the one shown in the following figure.

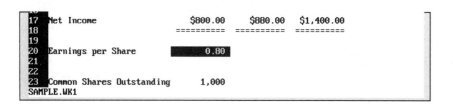

➤ **To copy the January Earnings per Share formula throughout the February through June columns:**

1.   Select **/C**opy.

2.   Type **B20** and press ⏎ to specify the range to copy FROM.

3.   Type **C20..G20** and press ⏎ to specify the range to copy TO.

     Check the results of your Copy command with the following figure.

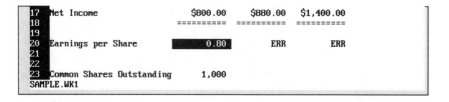

     Although not all incorrect calculations are marked, the results display *ERR* in the target cells to demonstrate that relative addressing used in the Copy command produced the wrong results.

4.   Move the cell pointer to cell C20.

Notice the formula (C17)/C23 displayed in the Control Panel for cell C20. The numerator C17 changed relative to position and is an accurate reference to February Net Income. The denominator C23 also changed relative to position and is inaccurate because it references an empty cell when it should continue referencing cell B23.

EDITING FORMULAS ➤ To correct the formula in cell B20 so that the numerator copies relative to position and the denominator copies the absolute reference to B23:

1.   Position the cell pointer in cell B20.

2.   Press the ⬚F2⬚ (EDIT) key.

The contents of cell B20 appear in the Control Panel area for editing. The Control Panel displays (B17)/B23, not the range names, to aid verification of proper cell reference.

3.   Position the cursor on the B in B23 and type **$**

4.   Position the cursor on the 2 in $B23 and type **$**

Check that your Control Panel matches the one shown in the following figure.

```
B20: (INCOME)/SHARES                                                    EDIT
 (B17)/$B$23
```

5.   Press ⏎ to enter the edited contents in cell B20.

➤ To copy the Earnings per Share formula with accurate results:

1.   Select /Copy.

2.   Type **B20** and press ⏎ to specify the range to copy FROM.

3.   Type **C20 . . G20** and press ⏎ to specify the range to copy TO.

Check that your results match those shown in row 20 in the following figure.

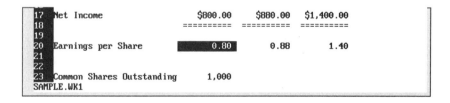

```
17 Net Income                    $800.00     $880.00   $1,400.00
18                              ==========   ========== ==========
19
20 Earnings per Share               0.80        0.88        1.40
21
22
23 Common Shares Outstanding      1,000
SAMPLE.WK1
```

➤ To clear the horizontal title fix and store the completed model under the same file name (replacing the expanded worksheet saved in an earlier example):

1. Select /**W**orksheet **T**itles **C**lear.

2. Press Home.

3. Select /**F**ile **S**ave.

4. Press ↵ to accept SAMPLE as the file name.

5. Select /**R**eplace.

INSERTING AND DELETING COLUMNS AND ROWS

Lotus 1-2-3 provides an Insert command to insert blank columns or rows within an existing worksheet. If one or more columns are inserted, existing data at the point of insertion shifts to the right. If one or more rows are inserted, existing data at the point of insertion shifts down. The letters for columns and the numbers for rows adjust to the new positions in the worksheet.

Lotus 1-2-3 also provides a **D**elete command to remove one or more columns or rows. Both commands require you to specify the point for insertion or deletion in terms of a range. If you prefer to type the insertion or deletion location, the cell pointer can be in any position. Otherwise, position the cell pointer in any cell within a row for row changes and in any cell within a column for column changes.

➤ To insert two rows:

1. Position the cell pointer in cell A2.

2. Select /**W**orksheet **I**nsert **R**ow.

3. At the "Enter row insert range:" prompt, press ↓ once and press ↵ to accept the range A2..A3.

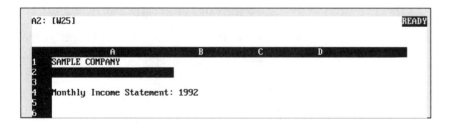

➤ To enter additional documentation and save the worksheet:

1. At cell A2 type **Midwest Division**

2. At cell A5 type **Prepared by:** (you can add your own name).

3. Save the current worksheet, updating the SAMPLE file on disk.

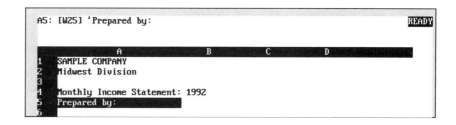

➤ To insert a column and format cells within the new column:

1. Position the cell pointer in cell A1.

2. Select /**W**orksheet **I**nsert **C**olumn and press ⏎ to insert one column in front of the existing column A.

3. Select /**R**ange **F**ormat **G**eneral.

4. Type **A1..A20** as the range to format and press ⏎.

    Check that your worksheet matches the one shown in the following figure.

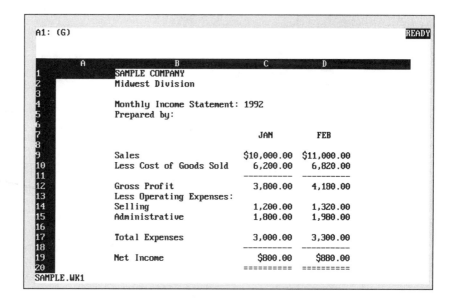

➤ To create data to erase in the next section:

1. Select /**D**ata **F**ill.

2. Type **A1..A20** and press ⏎ in response to the prompt for a fill range.

3. Type **1** as the start value and press ⏎.

4. Type **1** as the step value and press ⏎.

```
A1: (G)                                                              EDIT
Enter fill range: A1..A20
Start: 1                    Step: 1                    Stop: 8191
           A                 B                 C                 D
1                   SAMPLE COMPANY
2                   Midwest Division
3
```

5.   Press ↵ to accept the default 8191 maximum (your fill range will stop the generation of numbers at 20).

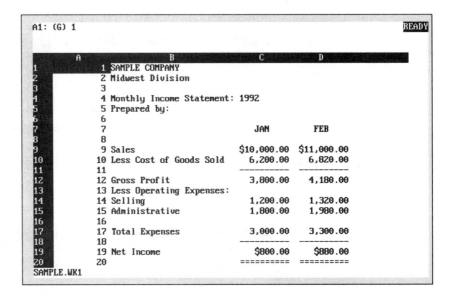

```
A1: (G) 1                                                            READY

           A                 B                 C                 D
       1 SAMPLE COMPANY
       2 Midwest Division
       3
       4 Monthly Income Statement: 1992
       5 Prepared by:
       6
       7                                  JAN        FEB
       8
       9 Sales                       $10,000.00  $11,000.00
      10 Less Cost of Goods Sold       6,200.00    6,820.00
      11                             ----------  ----------
      12 Gross Profit                  3,800.00    4,180.00
      13 Less Operating Expenses:
      14 Selling                       1,200.00    1,320.00
      15 Administrative                1,800.00    1,980.00
      16
      17 Total Expenses                3,000.00    3,300.00
      18                             ----------  ----------
      19 Net Income                     $800.00     $880.00
      20                             ==========  ==========
SAMPLE.WK1
```

The **Data Fill** command is a useful feature for entering any series of numbers that increment by a fixed amount, such as 5%, 10%, 15%; or $10,000, $20,000, $30,000; and so on.

ERASING CELL CONTENTS

In Project 1 you used the **/Worksheet Erase** command to produce a blank worksheet on the screen. Lotus 1-2-3 provides a similar command **/Range Erase** to remove data from specified cells. In contrast to the results of a **Delete Column** or **Delete Row** command, in which cells below and to the right of the point of deletion pack in, erased cells hold their position on the worksheet, but they are blank.

Caution: Be very careful when using the **Erase** or **Delete** commands, because mistakes in specifying ranges can be made very easily. Save your worksheet just prior to executing either command. If the **Erase** or **Delete** operation does not go as planned (e.g., erasing a column when you meant to erase a row), you can immediately retrieve the correct version on disk.

If you are using Release 2.2 or higher, you can activate the Undo feature, which allows you to reverse the last command. However, this feature requires a lot of memory to run.

➤ **To erase the contents of a specified range of cells:**

1. Select **/R**ange **E**rase.

2. Type **A1..A20** and press ⏎ in response to the prompt for a range to erase.

   The contents of cells A1..A20 disappear, but the blank cells hold their positions in column A of the worksheet. If you wanted both the data and the blank cells to be removed, you would execute a **D**elete **C**olumn command and specify any cell in column A.

➤ **To delete a column:**

1. Position the cell pointer in any cell within the column, in this case column A.

2. Select **/W**orksheet **D**elete **C**olumn.

3. Press ⏎ to delete the column at the current cell pointer location.

@FUNCTIONS

Lotus 1-2-3 contains a set of built-in formulas called functions. Many functions allow you to perform routinely used calculations more simply than if you had to use regular formulas.

Probably the most commonly used function is @SUM. Instead of having to enter a formula to add the values in cells B3, B4, B5, B6, C3, C4, C5, and C6 as B3+B4+B5+B6+C3+C4+C5+C6, you can specify the range of cells to add together as @SUM(B3..C6).

Date and time functions translate normal date and time formats (MM/DD/YY; HH:MM:SS) into serial numbers with which Lotus 1-2-3 can perform calculations. The @DATE function returns the serial date number of the year, month, and day. If you want to use the date June 25, 1993, in a calculation, enter the formula @DATE(93,6,25), and see the number "34145" returned as a serial number for that date. If June 26, 1993 had been specified, the serial number would increment by 1 to 34146.

The @NOW function will read the current date and time of your system. Every time Lotus 1-2-3 recalculates, the @NOW function is updated.

Other commonly used functions include the following:

@COUNT	Counts the number of nonblank entries in a specified list.
@ROUND	Rounds a number to the specified number of places.
@INT	Returns the integer part of the specified number.
@AVG	Returns the average of the values in a list.
@MIN	Returns the minimum value in a list.
@MAX	Returns the maximum value in a list.
@PMT	Computes the amount of periodic payment of a loan based on user-supplied values (or cell addresses) for the principal, periodic interest rate, and term of the loan.

Refer to the Lotus 1-2-3 reference manual for information on other @functions.

USING AN @FUNCTION TO DATE STAMP A WORKSHEET

There is a difference between creating worksheets and creating *effective* worksheets. In order for a worksheet to be useful, the contents must be easy to understand in addition to being accurate. You have already added to the clarity of the SAMPLE worksheet by indicating who developed the worksheet and inserting a subtitle to show the division to which the figures apply. Another item of information that should always be included is the date of preparation or last revision.

➤ **To enter a date using a Date function and select a Date format:**

1. Retrieve the SAMPLE worksheet if it is not the current worksheet.

2. At cell D5 type **@DATE(93,1,15)**

3. Select **/R**ange **F**ormat **D**ate.

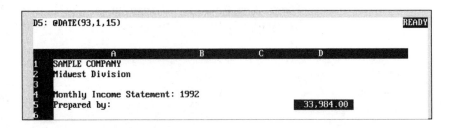

4. Select **1 (DD-MM-YY)**.

5. Type **D5** and press ↵ at the "Enter range to format:" prompt.

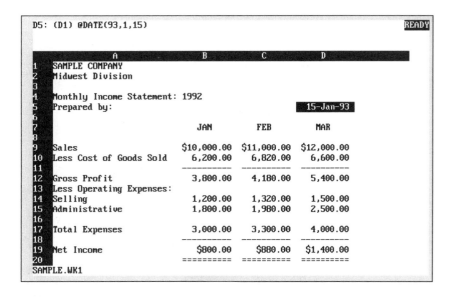

PRINTING WORKSHEET CONTENTS CELL BY CELL

Precautions should be taken to protect against loss of worksheet data. Make backup copies of all data files. In addition, use the **Cell-Formulas** print option to print a listing of cell contents and cell attributes (format, width, etc.), one cell to a line. If other security measures were to fail, you would at least have hard copy from which to reconstruct the worksheet.

➤ To print a list of actual cell contents:

1. Select **/P**rint **P**rinter.

2. Select **R**ange.

3. Type **A1..C12** and press ↵.

   You are printing only a portion of the worksheet contents to minimize print time. To properly document your own worksheets, include all cells that contain data.

4. Select **O**ptions **O**ther.

5. Select **C**ell-Formulas.

6. Select **Q**uit to return to the main printer menu.

7. Select **A**lign.

8. Select **G**o.

9. Select **P**age.

   Check that your output matches that shown in the following figure.

```
A1:   [W25] 'SAMPLE COMPANY
A2:   [W25] 'Midwest Division
A4:   [W25] 'Monthly Income Statement: 1992
A5:   [W25] 'Prepared by:
C5:   (D1) @DATE(93,1,15)
B7:   ^JAN
C7:   ^FEB
A9:   [W25] 'Sales
B9:   (C2) 10000
C9:   (C2) 11000
A10:  [W25] 'Less Cost of Goods Sold
B10:  6200
C10:  6820
B11:  "----------
C11:  "----------
A12:  [W25] 'Gross Profit
B12:  +B9-B10
C12:  +C9-C10
```

Each cell's contents are printed out one to a line arranged in column order, top to bottom, left to right. Only cells containing data appear on the list. Each line resembles what you see in line 1 of the Control Panel if you highlight the cell. For example, reading the first line, you learn that cell A1 has been set to a width of 25—[W25]—and contains the left-aligned label data SAMPLE COMPANY.

➤ **To reset a Print option to the default As-Displayed format:**

1. Select **O**ptions from the main printer menu.

2. Select **O**ther **A**s-Displayed to restore the default print format.

3. Select **Q**uit to restore the main printer menu.

4. Select **Q**uit to return to READY mode.

You may either continue with the Study Questions and Review Exercises or go on to Project 3. If you want to end this session, select **/Q**uit.

SUMMARY

- You specify a file name and drive\directory location to retrieve a file, just as you do to save a file.

- The **R**ange **L**abel command left-aligns, centers, or right-aligns the contents of a range of cells. Specify a range by highlighting the appropriate block on the screen or by typing the upper-left and lower-right coordinates separated by one or two periods.

- For a range that you reference frequently, consider assigning a range name for reference by a single word instead of pointing to or typing the range coordinates. Press ⌷F3⌷ when POINT mode is active, to see a list of range names defined in the current worksheet.

- As you develop your worksheets, you are likely to add or delete data. Lotus 1-2-3 allows you to insert rows and columns, delete rows and columns, and erase cell contents in a range, as well as move and copy data.

- Copy and Move commands both transfer data from a user-specified (FROM) source range to a user-specified (TO) target range. The former command retains the original data location and creates a second copy. The latter command transfers the original data to the new location.

- When you copy formulas containing cell references, the results in the target cells depend on your specification of addressing: relative to the starting position or absolute (fixed) at the starting position. Lotus 1-2-3 copies relative to position unless you precede a column letter or row number with a dollar sign ($).

- Normally changes to the current worksheet that have an impact on formulas cause the formulas to calculate automatically. You can speed the process when entering numerous changes to a large worksheet by setting the calculation to Manual until data entry is complete. Press ⟨F9⟩ to recalculate the worksheet when in Manual recalculation mode.

- As your worksheets increase in size, you may want to view separate portions on a single screen. Lotus 1-2-3 provides two menu options: Titles and Window. Execute a Titles command to freeze specified rows and/or columns on the screen. Select Window to split the screen in two parts horizontally or vertically.

- Make it a practice to insert documentation in your worksheets. Add titles to explain the purpose and contents of each worksheet, enter the name of the person(s) who developed the worksheet, and use an @DATE function to indicate the last day on which changes were made.

- You can produce documentation of another sort that allows you to reconstruct a worksheet from a hard copy printout of cell contents, one to a line. Use the Cell-Formulas option on the Print menus to produce this listing.

KEY TERMS

$ (dollar sign)	mixed address	source
absolute address	range	target
anchor	recalculate	
ERR	relative address	

STUDY QUESTIONS

TRUE/FALSE

1. Care should be given while typing labels, because their alignment cannot be changed without erasing the cell contents and typing the label again. T **(F)**

2. When a worksheet is retrieved, the incoming worksheet replaces the current worksheet in memory. T **(F)**

3. If you have not changed a default setting, copying a formula that contains a cell reference to a range of cells causes the cell references in the target range to be changed relative to the direction of the copy. T **(F)**

4. Typing a # symbol in front of the column and row in a cell reference will prevent that cell reference from changing during a copy operation. **(T)** F

5. The /Move operation moves data without regard to relative and absolute cell references. **(T)** F

6. Switching to Manual recalculation speeds the creation of large work-sheets. (T) **F**

7. If Insert is off when a column is inserted, the new column will replace the column where the cell pointer is located. (T) **F**

8. The phrase "date stamping" refers to leaving a group of cells empty to allow a date stamp to be affixed after printing. (T) **F**

9. To document a worksheet so that its contents can be retyped if necessary, list the contents by selecting the **C**ell by **C**ell Print option. (T) **F**

10. It is a good practice to save a worksheet before deleting rows and columns in case the wrong data is deleted. (T) **F**

FILL IN THE BLANKS

1. Type the ____#____ symbol in front of the column letter and row number to make sure that cell references are absolute.

2. The formula C12-D12 represents _3 row_ addressing.

3. To speed the creation of large worksheets, turn on _Manual_ recalculation.

4. The cell address C12 represents _\ col_ addressing.

5. Use the /**W**orksheet _____ command to view two separate portions of a worksheet without splitting the screen into two windows.

6. Use the _____ function to insert the current date into a cell.

7. Use the _____ Print format to display the contents of a range, one cell per line.

8. Press the _____ function key to recalculate a worksheet in Manual recalculation mode.

9. To duplicate the contents of a cell into another cell, and at the same time retain the original cell contents, use the / _____ command.

10. To duplicate the contents of a cell in another cell, and at the same time erase the original cell contents, use the / _____ command.

SHORT ANSWER

1. What is the purpose of a range name? What rules guide selection of a range name?

2. Discuss how the **W**indow option would help you develop or use a worksheet.

3. Discuss why you would print a worksheet using the cell by cell print format.

4. Describe how to insert a column between columns B and C.

5. Explain what changes need to be made to the formula D5*E5 to cause the reference to E5 not to be changed by a copy operation.

REVIEW EXERCISES

Continue to develop the Personal Property worksheet you created in the Project 1 Review Exercises.

1. Retrieve the PERSPROP worksheet.

2. Insert a column between columns A and B.

3. Create a column heading for the new column. Center the word **Date** in the new blank cell B4. Center the word **Acquired** in the new blank cell B5.

4. Use the @DATE function to enter the dates in column B that correspond to each item described in column A.

5. Move the worksheet title in A1 to B1.

6. Create a column heading for column E. Center the word **Change** in cell E4. Center the phrase **in Cost** in cell E5.

7. Enter the formula **+D6-C6** in cell E6.

8. Copy the formula to the remaining cells in column E that correspond to an item described in column A.

9. Verify the accuracy of the data and formulas, make necessary changes, and update the PERSPROP worksheet on disk.

10. Print the contents of the worksheet two ways: in a row-by-column format and in a cell-by-cell listing, one cell's contents and attributes to a line.

COMPETENCY TESTING

- Review the Topic Objectives to ensure you have mastered all skills listed.

- Ask your Class Assistant to check off:

  - Your completed Project work (the worksheet SAMPLE, the cell contents printout, and the first directory listing mentioned above).

  - Your completed True/False and Fill in the Blanks exercises.

  - Your completed Review Exercises (the worksheet PERSPROP, the two printouts, and your TDL).

- Ask your Class Assistant to see the **Modifying and Documenting a Worksheet**:

  - **Project Sample Sheet** to compare your work against the sample.

  - **True/False and Fill in the Blanks Correct Answer Sheet** to compare your answers against the correct ones.

  - **Review Exercises Sample Answer Sheet** to compare your work against it.

MANAGING THE ENVIRONMENT AND FILES

TOPIC OBJECTIVES
············

After completing this topic, you should be able to:

- Check worksheet status.
- View global default status.
- Change global defaults.
- Change the current directory temporarily.
- List file names of files stored on disk.
- Erase files from disk.
- Exit to DOS temporarily.

COMPUTER TUTORIAL
············

Managing the Environment and Files is a short topic. There are **no** tutorial activities for this topic, although you might want to review:

- From the **Novice** section:

  N Exit to DOS

PRACTICE EXERCISES
············

- Read and complete all **Project 3 work** outlined on pages 63 to 70:

  - Take special note of the **Key Terms** and **Summary** sections.

  - After the first bullet (" To create a practice file") under "Erasing Files" on page 69, *either*:

    Ask your Class Assistant to check your work;

    or, if you do this work outside of scheduled class time and your Class Assistant is not available, then you may:

    (alternatively) exit Lotus temporarily and prepare a directory listing in the same manner as you usually create your TDL. You can then ask your Class Assistant to check off the resulting printout.

- After finishing all Project work on pages 63 to 70, print a **directory listing** in the same manner as you usually create your TDL. This will be your *second* listing if you chose the second option, above.

- Do **True/False** exercises on page 71.

- Do **Fill in the Blanks** exercises on page 71.

- Do all **Review Exercises** on page 72, making sure you ask your Class Assistant to check off your work *after* Instruction 6 and *before* Instruction 7 so that both **123GONE.WK1** and **DOSGONE.WK1** show on your directory when your work is examined.

  If you do this work outside of scheduled class time when your Class Assistant is not available, you may alternatively exit Lotus temporarily *after* Instruction 6 and *before* Instruction 7, and prepare a directory listing in the same manner as you usually create your TDL. Then ask your Class Assistant to check off the resulting printout.

- Do the required **Topic Directory Listing (TDL).**

PROJECT 3: MANAGING THE ENVIRONMENT AND FILES

VIEWING WORKSHEET STATUS

The manner in which Lotus 1-2-3 operates is referred to as the Lotus 1-2-3 *environment.* It is important that you know how this environment is configured and how to change its settings temporarily or permanently. Two screens display most of the Lotus 1-2-3 environment, one showing worksheet *status* and the other giving printer and directory settings.

Selecting /**W**orksheet **S**tatus produces a full-screen report on worksheet-related global settings. If you are using Release 2.2 or higher, an almost identical screen appears when you select /**W**orksheet **G**lobal.

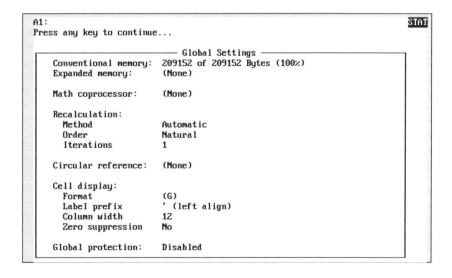

The information displayed includes available memory, recalculation mode, current global display settings (format, column width, etc.), and the status of cell protection (enabled or disabled). If cell protection is enabled, you cannot enter data into a cell unless the cell has been unprotected with a **R**ange command.

As you develop a large worksheet, check the amount of remaining memory before an error message appears advising you that there is insufficient memory. You might, for example, check the status of memory, disable the Undo feature (Release 2.2 or higher) to gain extra memory, and check the status again.

➤ **To view the worksheet status screen:**

1. Access a blank Lotus 1-2-3 worksheet.

2. Press **/** to access the Lotus 1-2-3 Main menu.

3. Select **W**orksheet **S**tatus.

4. Review the status information on your screen.

5. Press any key to continue, such as the space bar.

VIEWING GLOBAL DEFAULT STATUS

Selecting /**W**orksheet **G**lobal **D**efault **S**tatus produces a full-screen report that includes information about your printer and the default directory setup, as well as other defaults that affect screen messages and display of values.

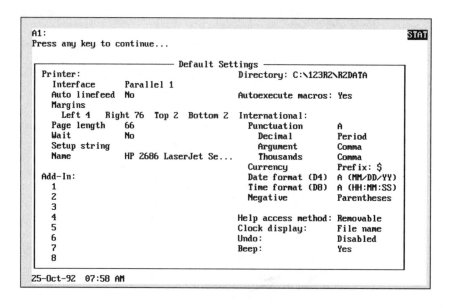

Printer information describes all of the current printer defaults, including which printer is selected for use. If your printing "creeps" down a page (each successive page in a multiple-page printout starts printing farther from the top than the previous page), this status screen might help. If you are using a laser printer and the page length is 66, changing the page length to 60 usually solves the problem.

Directory indicates what drive and directory are used for saving and retrieving files. In the previous figure, for example, data files are maintained in the \R2DATA subdirectory of the \123R2 directory on drive C:.

As you become more familiar with Lotus 1-2-3, many of the other settings displayed on the status screens will become meaningful.

➤ **To view the global default status screen:**

1. Select **/W**orksheet **G**lobal **D**efault **S**tatus.

2. Review the default information on your screen.

3. Press any key to restore the Global Default menu.

4. Select **Q**uit to restore READY mode.

CHANGING DEFAULT SETTINGS

You can quickly and easily change defaults through a series of menu selections. You must decide if you want to change a setting just for the current worksheet or for every worksheet you might develop. In the former situation, use a **W**orksheet **G**lobal menu option to change, for the current worksheet only, such settings as the global cell format, global label-prefix, global column-width, and recalculation mode. Worksheet-specific default settings will be saved when the worksheet is saved.

Default settings that pertain to the computer's hardware affect all worksheets. These settings can be saved as part of Lotus 1-2-3 and will remain in effect independently from specific worksheets. Using the **/W**orksheet **G**lobal **D**efault menu, you can specify settings for the printer, the default directory, and many other features.

You already experienced altering global settings when you specified a global column width of 12 or set recalculation to Manual. Additional exercises to change worksheet-related global settings are not provided. You will view the menus used to change printer and directory settings, but stop short of changing the specifications for your system.

➤ **To practice the steps to change the default directory:**

1. Select **/W**orksheet **G**lobal **D**efault.

2. Select **D**irectory.

   As shown in the following figure, a prompt to enter the default directory displays in the Control Panel. A flashing cursor appears at the end of the current drive\directory specification.

```
A1:                                                              EDIT
Enter default directory: C:\123R2\R2DATA
```

3. Imagine that you type a new directory path *(but do not type a new specification)*, and press ⏎.

4. Press ➡ to highlight **U**pdate.

```
A1:                                                           MENU
Printer  Directory  Status  Update  Other  Autoexec  Quit
Save new default settings in configuration file
```

Notice in the figure above, and on your screen, the explanation of the menu option that appears in line 3 of the Control Panel. Unless you select this option, the new setting only remains in effect during the current work session.

5.   Select **U**pdate.

The Default Settings menu remains on the screen.

➤ **To practice the steps to change the manner in which negative numbers display on the screen:**

1.   Select **O**ther from the Global Default menu.

2.   Select **I**nternational.

3.   Select **N**egative to view the two options available to display negative numbers.

```
A1:                                                           MENU
Parentheses  Sign
Display parentheses around negative numbers
```

You can display negative numbers within parentheses or preceded by a minus sign.

4.   Press [Ctrl]-[break] to abort the current command sequence and restore READY mode.

Through your brief exposure to changing global default settings in the previous exercises, you have an idea how to change the other settings. Just be sure to select **U**pdate before you quit the **G**lobal **D**efault menu or the changes will not be in effect the next time you turn on your computer.

If you work in a multi-user environment, be sure that you do not change settings that would adversely affect the work of other individuals. Any setting changed "permanently" through **G**lobal **D**efault menu selections can also be set "temporarily" through other means discussed later.

CHANGING THE DIRECTORY TEMPORARILY

Lotus 1-2-3 accesses a default directory that is set permanently, using the **W**orksheet **G**lobal **D**efault **D**irectory command, when performing the commands that refer to disk files. The default directory is usually set to a common directory that is used more often than others.

When you need to refer temporarily to another directory, you can type or select that directory each time you access a file. Typing or selecting a directory can be frustrating if you need to do it more than once. A solution is to temporarily change the default directory using the **/F**ile **D**irectory option. Temporary changes to a variety of directories can be made during the current edit session.

A setting established through a **File Directory** command always reverts to the global default when you exit Lotus 1-2-3.

➤ To set A:\ as the temporary default drive and directory:

1. Insert a formatted disk in drive A:.

2. Select **/File Directory**.

    Write down the directory information that displays in line 2 of the Control Panel, so that you can restore the original setting.

3. Type **A:** and press ⏎.

    If a disk was not inserted properly in drive A:, you would hear a beep, and the mode indicator would flash ERROR. Press Esc to clear an error message and repeat the process once a disk is in place.

➤ To verify that the temporary directory has been set:

1. Select **/File Retrieve**.

2. Check that your temporary directory reads "A:*.wk?"

3. Press Esc repeatedly or press Ctrl-[break] to restore READY mode.

➤ To reset the default directory:

1. Select **/File Directory**.

2. Enter the original directory and press ⏎.

LISTING FILES

Another option on the File menu allows you to see a *list* of files that are stored on disk. Lotus 1-2-3's **File List** command provides options to list all of the files in a directory, all files of a certain type, or selected file names. The file names are displayed in five columns across the screen, as shown in the following figure.

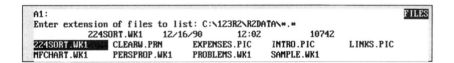

The first file name on the list is highlighted, and information about that file is displayed on the line above the list of names. Subdirectory names are included in any list of files. To see specific information—date, time, and file size—about any file, highlight the file name.

The File List menu contains a list of five field types from which to select. These types, determined by the extension portion of the file name, represent the files that you create while developing a worksheet. The five file types are shown below:

TYPE	EXTENSION	SOURCE
Worksheet	.WK1	Files created with **/File Save**.
Print	.PRN	Files created with **/Print File**.
Graph	.PIC	Files created with **/Graph Save**.
Other		All files in the directory.
Linked	.WK1	Files referred to in the current worksheet by linking formulas (Release 2.2 or higher).

The **/File List** option displays files in the default directory. You can also display additional files once the initial files appear on the screen.

TO DISPLAY	TAKE THIS ACTION
Selected files	Type the file name—wildcard characters are permitted.
A parent directory	Press [Backspace].
A subdirectory	Highlight the subdirectory name and press [↵].

➤ **To see a list of all worksheet (.WK?) files in the default directory:**

1. Select **/File List**.

2. Select **Worksheet**.

3. Highlight several file names and view the individual file information at the top of the screen.

4. Press [↵] to restore READY mode.

➤ **To see a list of all files in the default directory:**

1. Select **/File List**.

2. Select **Other**.

3. Press [↵] to restore READY mode.

ERASING FILES

When files are no longer needed, *erase* them from disk to free valuable space. Erasing files also eliminates the possibility that the wrong version of a worksheet will be used. Files can always be erased using the DOS DEL or ERASE commands. Lotus 1-2-3 also provides an Erase option, /File Erase.

Caution: Be careful when removing files from disk. Erased files cannot be undeleted in Lotus 1-2-3. Before deleting files from the current directory, make backup copies of important files that may be used in the future.

After selecting the **E**rase command, you have a choice of deleting from four file types: **W**orksheet, **P**rint, **G**raph, and **O**ther. Selecting a group limits the files that you will see on the screen to the specified file type. When you type or select the file name to be deleted, you see an on-screen warning to which you respond **N**o or **Y**es to complete the action.

Normally you will have no problem accumulating files to be deleted. However, to practice this process and avoid erasing an important file, create a file that can be deleted.

➤ **To create a practice file:**

1. Retrieve the SAMPLE worksheet.

2. Select /File **S**ave.

3. Type **ERASE-ME** and press ↵ to save the worksheet under another name.

➤ **To erase the ERASE-ME file from disk:**

1. Select /File **E**rase.

2. Select **W**orksheet.

3. Press F3 to see a full-screen display of file names.

4. Highlight ERASE-ME.WK1 and press ↵.

5. Select **Y**es to erase the worksheet.

➤ **To verify that the erase is complete:**

1. Select /File **L**ist **W**orksheet.

2. Check that the ERASE-ME worksheet does not appear on the list of files.

3. Press ↵ to restore READY mode.

EXITING TO DOS TEMPORARILY

Frequently your Lotus 1-2-3 editing session may be interrupted by the need to *exit* to DOS to perform some simple task. When this need arises, it is inconvenient to save your files and terminate the session. Instead, use the /**S**ystem command to temporarily suspend Lotus 1-2-3 and return to DOS.

When you are ready to return to Lotus 1-2-3, type **EXIT** and press ↵. If you type **123** or **Lotus** to get back into the program instead of **EXIT**, Lotus 1-2-3 will attempt to load a second time, and your system may freeze up or display an insufficient memory message. To clear the problem, reboot your system, which will cause any unsaved data to be lost. As a precaution, you may want to save your worksheet before exiting Lotus 1-2-3 through the **S**ystem option.

➤ To temporarily exit to DOS and execute a DOS command:

1. Select /**S**ystem.

   Check that your screen is similar to the one in the following figure.

```
(Type EXIT and press ENTER to return to 1-2-3)


Microsoft(R) MS-DOS(R)  Version 3.30
            (C)Copyright Microsoft Corp 1981-1987


C:\123R2>
```

2. Type **DIR** and press ⏎.

➤ To return to Lotus 1-2-3:

1. Type **EXIT** and press ⏎.

This concludes Project 3. You may either continue with the Study Questions and Review Exercises, or go on to the next topic. If you want to end this session, select /**Q**uit.

SUMMARY

- The Lotus 1-2-3 environment, which includes default settings, controls the manner in which the program operates.

- Two status reports are available in Lotus 1-2-3. The **W**orksheet **S**tatus command provides basic information about worksheet-related global settings; the **W**orksheet **G**lobal **D**efault **S**tatus command produces information about settings not specific to a worksheet, including printer and directory specifications.

- The **D**irectory option on the **F**ile menu is used to set the default directory for the duration of the editing session.

- Several other options on the **F**ile menu help you to manage your files without exiting Lotus 1-2-3, including **L**ist, to view files; and **E**rase, to remove files no longer needed.

- The /**S**ystem option suspends processing, allowing you to temporarily return to DOS. Type **EXIT** to return to the program at precisely the operation where processing was suspended.

KEY TERMS

environment	exit	status
erase	list	

STUDY QUESTIONS

TRUE/FALSE

1. The way Lotus 1-2-3 operates, using a series of defaults, is often referred to as the Lotus 1-2-3 environment. (T) F

2. The /Worksheet Global Default menu contains global options that can be set only for the current worksheet. T (F)

3. To temporarily set the default directory, use the /Worksheet Global Default Directory command. T (F)

4. When you access a directory that does not contain files, Lotus 1-2-3 automatically switches to EDIT mode. T (F)

5. Lotus 1-2-3 allows you to list file names by file type. (T) F

6. The /Files List command displays the file names in five columns across the screen. (T) F

7. Files that are removed using the /Files Erase command can be undeleted if action is taken before exiting Lotus 1-2-3. (T) F

8. Before erasing a file, you are prompted No or Yes to confirm removing the file from disk. (T) F

9. When temporarily exiting to DOS, it is not necessary to save the current worksheet. T (F)

10. To return to Lotus 1-2-3 after exiting to DOS with a /System command, type **LOTUS** and press ↵. T (F)

FILL IN THE BLANKS

1. The Lotus 1-2-3 environment includes a series of _global_ settings, which you can change.

2. Settings on the /Worksheet Global _Default_ menu are set permanently or until they are changed again.

3. To remove files from disk within Lotus 1-2-3, use the /File _Erase_ command.

4. To set a temporary directory, use the /File _DIR_ command.

5. When you access a directory that has no files, you are automatically in _Ready_ mode.

6. When listing files in the current directory, you can also see files in the parent directory by pressing _Backspace_.

7. After initiating a File Erase command, you can press _LIST_ to see a full-screen display of file names.

8. To exit Lotus 1-2-3 temporarily, use the _System_ command.

9. To return to Lotus 1-2-3 after temporarily exiting to DOS, type _Exit_ .

10. The /Worksheet _Status_ option displays the cell-related global settings.

SHORT ANSWER

1. Differentiate between the terms "global" and "default."

2. Discuss how you temporarily exit Lotus 1-2-3 and return. Give two examples why you might temporarily exit Lotus 1-2-3.

3. Describe how you list files from Lotus 1-2-3, and include the process for displaying files from the parent directory.

4. Discuss how files can be erased from Lotus 1-2-3.

5. Describe how to set the default directory permanently and temporarily.

REVIEW EXERCISES

1. Load your PERSPROP.WK1 worksheet into memory and display the current worksheet status.

2. Display the Lotus 1-2-3 default status set by the Global Default menu.

3. Using the Global Default menu, change the display so that the current worksheet name appears in the lower-left corner of the screen. If the screen already displays the worksheet name, display the date and time. When you have viewed both settings, select the setting that you prefer.

4. Display a list of all worksheet files in the current directory.

5. Display a list of all files in the current directory.

6. Access a blank worksheet and type **This is a practice worksheet** in cell A1. Save the current worksheet as 123GONE.WK1. Repeat the **S**ave process, saving the current worksheet as DOSGONE.WK1.

7. Using a **F**ile command, erase the 123GONE.WK1 worksheet from disk.

8. Temporarily exit Lotus 1-2-3 to DOS and erase the DOSGONE.WK1 file. When you finish erasing the file, return to Lotus 1-2-3.

COMPETENCY TESTING

• Review the Topic Objectives to ensure you have mastered all skills listed.

• Ask your Class Assistant to check off:

- Your Project work (in-process *or* the printed directory listing mentioned in the Practice Exercises section).

- Your completed True/False and Fill in the Blanks exercises.

- Your completed Review Exercises and your TDL. As noted above, check-off has to happen *after* Instruction 6 and *before* Instruction 7 so that both 123GONE.WK1 and DOSGONE.WK1 show on your directory when your work is examined (note the alternative suggested in the Practice Exercises section, above, for preparing material for check-off if you do this work outside of scheduled class time).

• Ask your Class Assistant to see the **True/False and Fill in the Blanks Correct Answer Sheet** for this topic and compare your answers against the correct ones.

TOPIC OBJECTIVES

·············

After completing this topic, you should be able to:

- Extract a portion of a worksheet to a disk file.

- Combine all or part of a worksheet into another worksheet.

  - Expand a worksheet by incorporating existing data from another worksheet.

- Remove numbers from a worksheet, retaining labels and formulas.

  - Create a reusable worksheet by removing only numeric data.

- Display name of current worksheet on screen (in place of clock display).

- Use formulas to link worksheets.

- Use @SUM.

COMPUTER TUTORIAL

·············

- From the **Advanced** section, work through:

  B   Combine worksheets (treat material on sorting as optional)

PRACTICE EXERCISES

·············

- Read and complete all **Project 4 work** outlined on pages 74 to 85:

  - Take special note of the **Key Terms** and **Summary** sections.

  - Be sure to save the files **SAMPLE** (pages 74 and 75), **YTD** (page 77), **YTDMODEL** (pages 78 and 79), **INDPLS** (pages 80 and 81), **COLUMBUS** (pages 81 and 82), **LINKS** (pages 82 and 83) and **LINKS2** (page 84).

- After finishing all Project work on pages 74 to 85, print a **directory listing** in the same manner as you usually create your TDL.

- Do **True/False** exercises on page 86.

- Do **Fill in the Blanks** exercises on pages 86 and 87.

- Do all Review Exercises on pages 87 and 88, making sure to save **TOTHOURS**, **FALL92**, **SPRING93**, **FALL93**, and **TOTHRS2**.

- Do the required **Topic Directory Listing (TDL)**.

NOTE
- In the Project work, when you save SAMPLE on pages 74 and 75, note that this is a replacement of SAMPLE: be sure you have already had the previous version checked off by your Class Assistant.

PROJECT 4: WORKING WITH MULTIPLE WORKSHEETS

EXTRACTING PART OF A WORKSHEET TO DISK

As you develop increasingly large and complex worksheets, there may be occasions when you would like to work with only a portion of the data in a separate file. Lotus 1-2-3 provides a **File X**tract command that allows you to copy a typed or named range from the current worksheet to a disk file. The extracted portion of the worksheet remains part of the original work and also appears in a new smaller worksheet file on disk.

You have the option of *extracting* the range as Formulas or Values, a choice that affects only cells containing formulas. An example will explain the difference. Suppose you had a worksheet that included the following formula and numbers in the range A1..A3.

CELL	CONTENTS	DISPLAY
A1	20	20
A2	25	25
A3	+A1+A2	45

If you extracted the range A1..A3 as formulas, cell A3 in the new worksheet on disk would contain the formula +A1+A2. If you extracted the range A1..A3 as values, cell A3 in the new worksheet would contain the number 45.

You can practice the process by extracting in four separate operations the column A descriptions and the January, February, and March data in columns B through D from the SAMPLE worksheet. You will use the extracted files in a subsequent exercise on combining files.

➤ **To name the January, February, and March data ranges in the SAMPLE worksheet and save the changes:**

1. Retrieve the SAMPLE worksheet.

2. Select **/R**ange **N**ame **C**reate.

3. Type **JAN** at the "Enter name:" prompt and press ↵.

4. Type **B9..B20** at the "Enter range:" prompt and press ↵.

5. Repeat steps 2 through 4, but specify a **FEB** range **C9..C20**

6. Repeat steps 2 through 4, but specify a **MAR** range **D9..D20**

7. Select /**F**ile **S**ave.

8. Press ⏎ to update the SAMPLE file on disk.

9. Select **R**eplace at the "Cancel Replace Backup" prompt.

➤ **To extract the descriptive information from column A in the SAMPLE worksheet and create a new worksheet named YTD on disk:**

1. Select /**F**ile **X**tract.

2. Select **V**alues or **F**ormulas.

   You can select either option, because the **F**ormulas and **V**alues options vary in effect on formula cells only and the range you are going to extract does not contain any formulas.

3. Type **YTD** at the "Enter name of file to extract to:" prompt and press ⏎.

4. Type **A1..A20** at the "Enter extract range:" prompt and press ⏎.

COMBINING WORKSHEETS

When expanding a worksheet, you may realize that you already have most or all of the new data on disk in another worksheet. Incorporating existing data could save a lot of time. However, if you use a File Retrieve command to load a second worksheet, the one previously in memory will disappear.

To include data from another worksheet in the current worksheet, use the File Combine feature. Three options are available: Copy, Add, and Subtract.

The **C**opy option loads the specified data on disk into the current worksheet, starting at the current *cell pointer position*. Be sure that the current cell pointer position marks the upper-left corner of a blank area that is large enough to hold the *incoming range*. If data already exists in the *target area*, it will be overwritten by the *incoming data*.

Choosing the **A**dd option in the File Combine sequence causes any numeric information in the specified incoming data to be added to data already present in the target cells. The position of the cell pointer upon initiation of the command again marks the upper-left corner of the range where incoming data will be combined with existing data. For example, if a Combine Add operation combines an incoming cell containing the number 15 with a cell on the current worksheet containing the number 12, the result will be 27. Two common uses for this feature include accumulating year-to-date information and consolidating financial reports of various departments, projects, divisions, and so on.

It may sound inconsistent to select **S**ubtract after initiating a File Combine command sequence, but the option is quite powerful in two primary ways. First, you can use the feature to reduce all numbers to zero but retain labels and formulas. The result is a worksheet model that can be used to enter new data, such as data for the next year. For this use, specify the name of the current worksheet when prompted for a file name, in order for the file to be subtracted from itself.

Second, you can use the File Combine Subtract sequence to undo a previous File Combine Add. For example, suppose you executed a File Combine Add command and the cell pointer was not in the correct position, resulting in incorrect summary figures or data overlaid in inappropriate places. You can immediately subtract the named file and undo the damage.

After selecting among the Copy, Add, and Subtract options, you are prompted to specify the incoming data as being an entire file or a named range (for Release 2.0 and higher, you can also type your range specifications).

To become familiar with the concepts, let's use the Copy and Add options to create a worksheet that contains year-to-date information summarizing the monthly data found in the SAMPLE worksheet. First retrieve the descriptive information in column A that was previously extracted to the file named YTD. Next combine, one at a time, the named ranges of data for January, February, and March (although only three months of data are used to illustrate the procedures, you can continue the process each month, updating the YTD worksheet).

➤ **To retrieve the newly extracted file named YTD, add a heading, and copy January data into the current worksheet:**

1. Retrieve the YTD worksheet.

2. Position the cell pointer in cell B7.

3. Type **^YTD** and press ⏎ to center a heading for the column that will be used to accumulate monthly data.

4. Position the cell pointer in cell B9.

5. Select /File Combine Copy Named/Specified-Range.

6. Type **JAN** at the "Enter the range name or address:" prompt and press ⏎.

7. Type **SAMPLE** at the "Enter the name of the file to combine:" prompt and press ⏎.

    Check that your screen matches the one shown in the following figure.

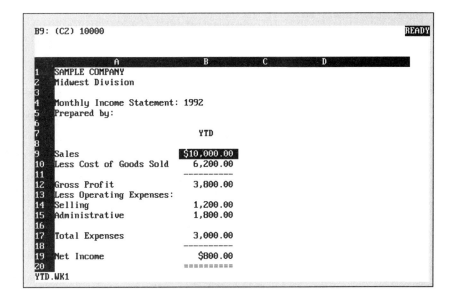

➤ **To update the YTD worksheet to include February and March figures stored on disk:**

1. Position the cell pointer in cell B9.

2. Select /**F**ile **C**ombine **A**dd **N**amed/Specified-Range.

3. Type **FEB** at the "Enter the range name or address:" prompt and press ⏎.

4. Type **SAMPLE** at the "Enter the name of the file to combine:" prompt and press ⏎.

5. Repeat steps 1 through 4 to add the March figures from the SAMPLE worksheet.

   Check that your screen display matches the one shown in the following figure.

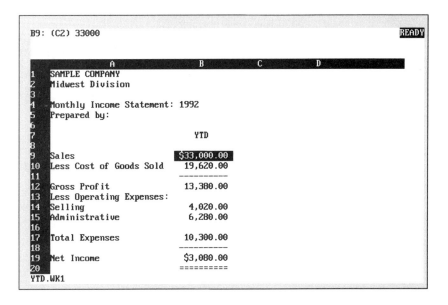

6. Save the current YTD worksheet (be sure to select **R**eplace when prompted).

➤ **To practice the process of using Combine Subtract to undo the effects of a previous Combine Add by subtracting the March data from the current YTD worksheet:**

1. Position the cell pointer in cell B9.

2. Select /File Combine Subtract Named/Specified-Range.

3. Type **MAR** at the "Enter the range name or address:" prompt and press ⏎.

4. Type **SAMPLE** at the "Enter the name of the file to combine:" prompt and press ⏎.

   Check that your YTD worksheet matches the one shown in the following figure.

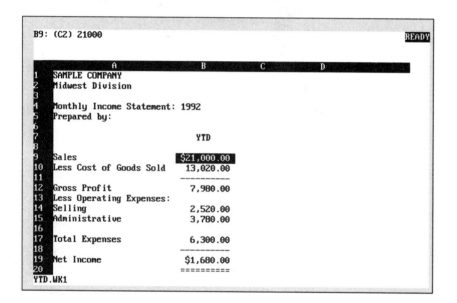

➤ **To create a reusable worksheet model by removing all numeric data using Combine Subtract:**

1. Retrieve the YTD file stored on disk, which contains the JAN, FEB, and MAR accumulated balances.

2. Position the cell pointer in cell A1.

3. Select /File Combine Subtract.

4. Select Entire-File.

5. Type **YTD** at the "Enter the name of the file to combine:" prompt and press ⏎.

   Check that your screen matches the one shown in the following figure.

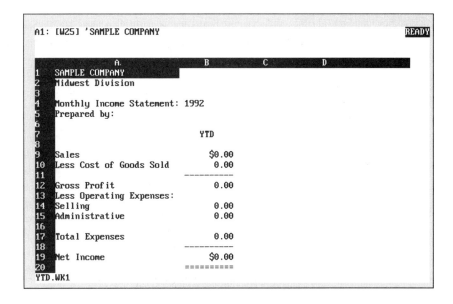

If your screen does not match, you may not have had the cell pointer in the proper position before executing the command. Retrieve the YTD worksheet and repeat steps 2 through 5.

6. Move the cell pointer throughout your screen display and note that only label and formula entries remain.

7. Save the current YTD worksheet as YTDMODEL.

You could have used several **R**ange **E**rase commands to remove numeric data from the small worksheet used in previous exercises. However, stripping numeric data from a very large worksheet is much easier using a single **F**ile **Com**bine **S**ubtract command as opposed to numerous **R**ange **E**rase commands.

If you were careful to follow previous instructions, your **F**ile **C**ombine activities worked exactly as intended. However, mistakes occur, such as failing to position the cell pointer appropriately, or selecting **S**ubtract when you meant to select **A**dd. As a precaution, consider saving the current worksheet before you initiate a **C**ombine operation. If the results are thoroughly jumbled, you can retrieve the current worksheet and start over.

LINKING WORKSHEETS

One powerful new feature of Lotus 1-2-3 Release 2.2 (or higher) is the ability to link worksheets using formulas in the current worksheet. You are no longer limited to consolidating figures from several worksheets using a **F**ile **C**ombine **C**opy or **A**dd command. There are dozens of applications that are made simpler by this feature.

Formulas that reference a cell from another worksheet include the name of the worksheet within double angle brackets. For example, the formula +<<INDPLS.WK1>>F4 references the contents of cell F4 in the INDPLS.WK1 worksheet, when INDPLS.WK1 is not the current worksheet. When entering a formula, remember to start with a number or one of the numeric symbols—in this case, the + symbol. The next portion of the sample formula, <<INDPLS.WK1>>, indicates the worksheet you want to link to the current worksheet. The double brackets enclose the name of a file on disk. Finally, the

F4 in the formula refers to cell F4 in the INDPLS.WK1 worksheet, whose contents are to be brought forward into the current worksheet.

Lotus 1-2-3 Release 2.2 does not permit you to use the +<<INDPLS.WK1>>F4 formula inside another formula. Therefore, you cannot link two or more formulas together and summarize multiple worksheets or cells into a single cell.

Once the formula is entered in a cell, the contents from the linked worksheet appear immediately. However, if the contents of the linked cell—F4 in INDPLS.WK1—change, the current cell will not be updated automatically. You can list all files linked to a worksheet using the **File List Linked** command. When retrieving a worksheet that contains linking formulas, it is a good practice to refresh those cells using the **/File Admin Link-refresh** command.

The process of linking files is not as complicated as it might seem. Creating your own application will make the concepts more easily understood. Imagine that you own several golf courses. The manager of each golf course prepares an estimate of next year's revenue, by the sources of income for each quarter. Each estimated revenue statement is sent to you to be summarized into a master worksheet representing all of your golf courses.

Two worksheets, saved in separate files, represent revenue statements for Indianapolis Links (stored on disk as the file INDPLS.WK1) and Columbus Links (stored on disk as COLUMBUS.WK1). The worksheet names are important, because they will be used as part of the cell reference when linking worksheets.

Because you will be working with several worksheets, display the current worksheet name in the lower-left corner of the screen. When you do this, the date will continue to display on the screen until you save the worksheet or retrieve a worksheet into memory.

➤ To display the current file name on screen:

1. Select **/W**orksheet **G**lobal **D**efault.

2. Check the setting for "Clock display:" in the lower-right corner. If the setting is "File name," go to step 4.

3. Select **O**ther **C**lock **F**ilename.

4. Select **Q**uit to restore READY mode.

➤ To create a Revenue Statement for Indianapolis Links:

1. Study the worksheet in the following figure.

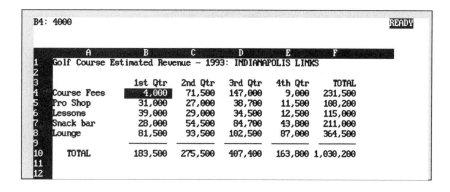

2. Set column A to a width of 15.

3. Set the global column width to 10 (or the individual column widths for columns B, C, D, E, and F to 10).

4. Enter the labels in cells A1, B3..F3, A4..A10, and B9..F9.

5. Enter the numbers shown in cells B4..E8.

6. Enter formulas into cells F4..F8 that sum the numbers in their respective cells.

7. Enter formulas in cells B10..F10 that sum the numbers in their respective columns.

8. Select **/F**ile **S**ave.

9. Type **INDPLS** and press ⏎ to save the worksheet to disk.

To save time and typing, you can use the current INDPLS.WK1 to create the next worksheet. To do this, save the current worksheet immediately as COLUMBUS.WK1, make changes to the estimated revenue figures, and save the changes.

➤ To create a Revenue Statement for Columbus Links:

1. Check that the INDPLS worksheet is the current worksheet.

2. Select **/F**ile **S**ave.

3. Type **COLUMBUS** and press ⏎ to save the worksheet to disk as a new worksheet.

4. Study the worksheet in the following figure.

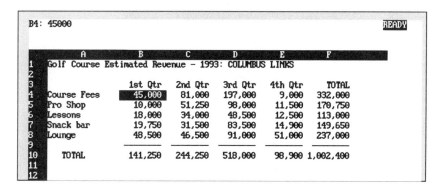

5. Position the cell pointer in cell A1.

6. Press F2 to access EDIT mode, and display the contents of cell A1 on the second line of the Control Panel for edit.

7. Edit the title to read COLUMBUS LINKS instead of INDIANAPOLIS LINKS and press ⏎.

8. Enter the values shown in the previous figure for cells B4..E8 into the corresponding cells on the current COLUMBUS worksheet.

9. Select /File Save.

10. Press ⏎ and select Replace to update the COLUMBUS file on disk.

Study the worksheet in the following figure illustrating the consolidated estimated revenue worksheet called LINKS, which you are going to create. Refer frequently to this figure during the creation process.

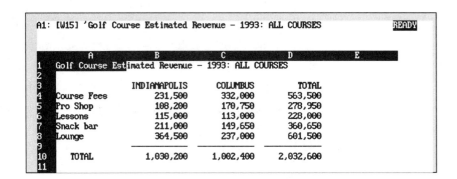

Creating a summary worksheet for both golf courses and pulling data from each worksheet you just created are simple tasks that involve only one new technique. However, before linking worksheets, first create a summary worksheet. To save time and typing, you can use portions of the current COLUMBUS.WK1 worksheet to create the summary worksheet named LINKS.

➤ **To create the descriptive labels in the worksheet:**

1. Check that COLUMBUS is the current worksheet.

2. Press Home to position the cell pointer at cell A1.

3. Press /File Xtract Formulas.

4. Type **LINKS** and press ⏎.

5. When prompted to "Enter extract range:" type **A1..A10** and press ⏎.

6. Select /File Retrieve.

7. Select LINKS.WK1.

Check that your screen matches the one shown in the following figure.

```
A1: [W15] 'Golf Course Estimated Revenue - 1993: COLUMBUS LINKS      READY

           A         B        C        D        E        F
1   Golf Course Estimated Revenue - 1993: COLUMBUS LINKS
2
3
4   Course Fees
5   Pro Shop
6   Lessons
7   Snack bar
8   Lounge
9
10      TOTAL
11
12
13
```

8. Edit the contents of cell A1 to read "Golf Course Estimated Revenue - 1993: ALL COURSES."

9. Widen columns B and C to 14 characters.

10. Enter into the current worksheet the column headings in cells B3..D3 and the separator lines in cells B9..D9, as shown in the following figure.

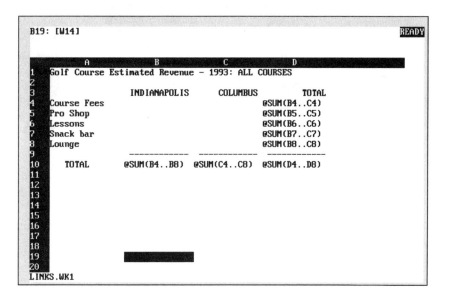

```
B19: [W14]                                                           READY

           A              B              C              D
1   Golf Course Estimated Revenue - 1993: ALL COURSES
2
3                     INDIANAPOLIS      COLUMBUS          TOTAL
4   Course Fees                                        @SUM(B4..C4)
5   Pro Shop                                           @SUM(B5..C5)
6   Lessons                                            @SUM(B6..C6)
7   Snack bar                                          @SUM(B7..C7)
8   Lounge                                             @SUM(B8..C8)
9                    ------------   ------------   ------------
10      TOTAL        @SUM(B4..B8)   @SUM(C4..C8)   @SUM(D4..D8)
11
12
13
14
15
16
17
18
19
20
LINKS.WK1
```

Study the worksheet in the previous figure before entering the formulas, to summarize worksheet values, in order to understand what each formula calculates.

start Nov 18/94

▶ **To enter the @SUM formulas in the summary worksheet:**

1. Enter the formula @SUM(B4..C4) in cell D4 and copy the formula to the range D5..D8.

2. Enter the formula @SUM(B4..B8) in cell B10 and copy the formula to the range C10..D10.

3. Select /File Save and press ⏎ to update the LINKS worksheet on disk.

The worksheet in the following figure shows the formulas for pulling figures from two other worksheets into the current worksheet. Notice that references to two worksheets are made within double angle brackets, INDPLS.WK1 and COLUMBUS.WK1.

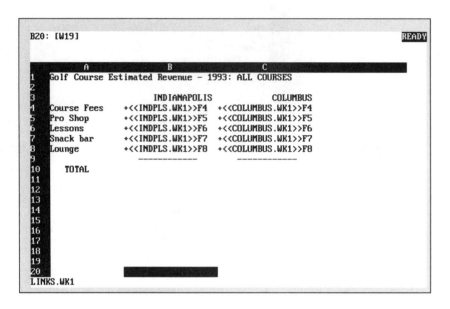

➤ **To enter formulas that link two worksheets to the current summary worksheet and save that worksheet:**

1. At cell B4, type **+<<INDPLS.WK1>>F4** and press ⏎.

2. Copy the formula in cell B4 to the range B5..B8.

3. At cell C4, type **+<<COLUMBUS.WK1>>F4** and press ⏎.

4. Copy the formula in cell C4 to the range C5..C8.

   Check that your screen matches the one shown in the following figure.

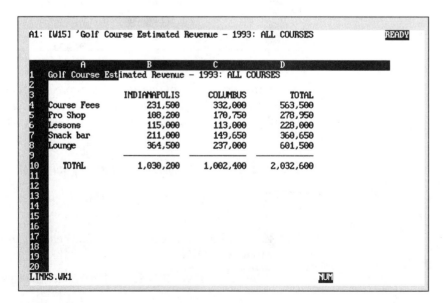

5. Select /**F**ile **S**ave.

6. Type **LINKS2** and press ⏎ to save the linked worksheet to disk.

This brief exercise allows you to glimpse the power of being able to work with more than one worksheet at a time. Lotus 1-2-3 Release 3 and higher greatly simplifies the process of linking worksheets by allowing you to have multiple worksheets in memory instead of just one.

This concludes Project 4. You may either continue with the Study Questions and Review Exercises or go on to the next topic. If you want to end the session, select /**Q**uit.

SUMMARY

- Lotus 1-2-3 provides a **F**ile **X**tract command to copy a portion of a worksheet to disk as a separate worksheet file. Formulas within the copied portion can appear as formulas or the values produced by the formulas in the new worksheet.

- If you want to retrieve all or part of a worksheet stored on disk into the worksheet currently in memory, use a **F**ile **C**ombine command instead of a **F**ile **R**etrieve command.

- Three options are available when using the **F**ile **C**ombine command: **C**opy, **A**dd, and **S**ubtract.

- The **F**ile **C**ombine **C**opy command is used to retrieve data into a blank area of the current worksheet.

- The **F**ile **C**ombine **A**dd command can be used to accumulate amounts, such as year-to-date sales and expenses.

- The **F**ile **C**ombine **S**ubtract command is primarily used to strip numbers from a worksheet, retaining the labels and formulas as a model that can be stored for future use.

- One of Lotus 1-2-3's powerful new features in Release 2.2 or higher is the ability to use formulas to bring data from other worksheets into the current worksheet.

- Formulas that link worksheets contain a reference to the linked file name and cell in the form +<<worksheet>>cell.

- Once a formula is linked, it must be refreshed each time the worksheet is used to ensure that the linked cells are current.

- When working with multiple worksheets, it is helpful to display the current file name in the lower-left corner of the screen instead of the date and time.

KEY TERMS

cell pointer position	extracting values	incoming range
extracting formulas	incoming data	target area
extracting ranges		

STUDY QUESTIONS

TRUE/FALSE

1. Linking worksheets refers to formulas in the current worksheet that refer to cells in another worksheet. **(T)** **F**

2. The name of the file that is being linked in a formula is enclosed in double brackets: [[and]]. **T** **(F)**

3. The data in the current or target worksheet will automatically be updated when the data in a linked worksheet is changed. **T** **(F)**

4. A range of cells in the current worksheet can be extracted and placed in a new worksheet on disk. **(T)** **F**

5. One limitation of the File **X**tract command is that only the values of a cell (not the formulas) are extracted to the new worksheet. **(T)** **F**

6. The **X**tract option is a convenient way to erase portions of the current worksheet. **(T)** **F**

7. When combining two worksheets using the **C**opy option of the File Combine command, the incoming cell contents copy over the corresponding cells in the current worksheet. **(T)** **F**

8. The range being combined from disk is placed in the current worksheet beginning at the location of the cell pointer. **T** **(F)**

9. The **C**ombine **S**ubtract operation causes the numbers in the respective cells to be subtracted. **T** **(F)**

10. Always position the cell pointer at cell A1 before you execute a File Combine command. **(T)** **F**

FILL IN THE BLANKS

1. To make sure that the contents of linked cells are current, you should _____ the linked cells.

2. To link cell A1 in the SAMPLE worksheet on disk to a different worksheet currently in memory, type the formula _____.

3. When using multiple worksheets, it is useful to display the current ___File___ name in the lower left corner of the screen.

4. To add the contents of two worksheets together, use the ___Add___ command.

5. Combined data is inserted in the current worksheet, beginning at the location of the ___last___ cell.

6. A range of data being extracted can be referred to by its cell address or a _____ name.

7. When combining files, if you use the ___Combine___ option, the whole worksheet will be combined with the current worksheet.

8. If the extracted file name is already on disk, you will be prompted to cancel the extract or _____ the file.

9. When you specify a range to extract, the range cannot include formulas that reference cells _____ the extracted range.

10. The /File Combine ___Add___ option replaces the entries in the current worksheet with incoming cells.

SHORT ANSWER

1. Discuss the concept of linking multiple worksheets.

2. Describe an application for linking worksheets.

3. Describe an application for extracting part of a worksheet to a new file.

4. Describe an application for combining worksheets using the **C**opy and **A**dd options.

5. Discuss which feature (linking, combining, or extracting) you would use to create the shell of a new worksheet from an existing worksheet.

REVIEW EXERCISES

1. Create four small worksheets so you can practice the /File Combine operations.

   Create and save a worksheet shell called TOTHOURS that includes the entries (columns A and B and rows 1 through 4) shown below.

	A	B
1	Student	CreditHrs
2	A	
3	B	
4	C	

   Add the data shown next in cells B2, B3, and B4 and save the worksheet as FALL92.

	A	B
1	Student	CreditHrs
2	A	17
3	B	14
4	C	15

   Modify the data in cells B2 and B4 as shown below and save the worksheet as SPRING93.

	A	B
1	Student	CreditHrs
2	A	19
3	B	14
4	C	17

   Modify the data in cells B3 and B4 as shown below and save the worksheet as FALL93.

	A	B
1	Student	CreditHrs
2	A	19
3	B	16
4	C	15

2. Use **File Combine** commands to produce a worksheet that displays the total credit hours to date for each student in the range B2..B4. TOTHOURS should be used for this **Combine** operation. Be sure to save (replace) it after the **Combine**.

3. If you are using Lotus 1-2-3 Release 2.2 or higher, enter a formula to calculate the total credit hours of student A by linking three worksheets. Save the worksheet that results from this linking as TOTHRS2.

 # COMPETENCY TESTING
....

- Review the Topic Objectives to ensure you have mastered all skills listed.

- Ask your Class Assistant to check off:

  - Your Project work (the printed directory listing mentioned above in the Practice Exercises section and worksheets created).

  - Your completed True/False and Fill in the Blanks exercises.

  - Your completed Review Exercises (TOTHOURS, TOTHRS2, and your TDL).

- Ask your Class Assistant to see the **Working with Multiple Worksheets**:

  - **Project Sample Sheet** to compare your work against the samples.

  - **True/False and Fill in the Blanks Correct Answer Sheet** to compare your answers against the correct ones.

  - **Review Exercises Sample Answer Sheet** to compare your work against it.

GRAPHING DATA

TOPIC OBJECTIVES

After completing this topic, you should be able to:

- Identify a graph's type: line, bar, XY, stacked bar, or pie.
- Select an appropriate graph type.
- Create and enhance a graph (titles, scale, grid).
- View graph on screen.
- Store graph specifications within the associated worksheet ("name" the graph).
- Create a pie chart.
- Save a graph as a .PIC file that can be printed ("save" the graph).
- Save current worksheet, including named graphs.
- Print a graph using PrintGraph (preview, select size and style).
- Add a legend to a graph.

COMPUTER TUTORIAL

- From the **Novice** section, work through:

  K Graph your data

  M Print with Lotus 1-2-3 (half of option M, as follows):
  - Use the PrintGraph program
  - Select a graph
  - Select a type style
  - Print a graph

PRACTICE EXERCISES

- Read and complete all **Project 5 work** outlined on pages 90 to 102:
  - Take special note of the **Key Terms** and **Summary** sections.
  - Be sure to name and save the graphs **DEMOBAR** and **PIE** and save the worksheet **SAMPLE**.

- After finishing all Project work on pages 90 to 102, print a **directory listing** in the same manner as you usually create your TDL.

- Do **True/False** exercises on page 102.

- Do **Fill in the Blanks** exercises on pages 102 and 103.

- Do all **Review Exercises** on page 103, making sure to name, save, and print the graphs **LINE.PIC** and **TWOBAR.PIC**.

- Do the required **Topic Directory Listing (TDL).**

PROJECT 5: GRAPHING DATA

DECIDING WHICH TYPE OF GRAPH TO USE

Lotus 1-2-3 offers five types of graphs: line, bar, XY, stacked bar, and pie. Although you can use any type of graph as long as you specify the appropriate data range, certain graphs are generally used to illustrate certain kinds of information.

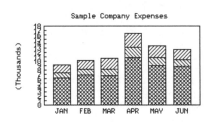

a) Stacked Bar Graph

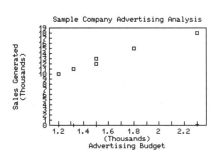

b) XY Graph

c) Pie Chart

d) Line Graph

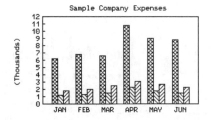

e) Bar Graph

A *line graph* shows changes in data over time. A *bar graph* compares sets of data. Lotus 1-2-3 is capable of producing single-range or multiple-range bar graphs. An *XY graph* illustrates the relationship between two sets of data. A *stacked bar graph* is similar to a bar graph, but instead of comparing single sets of data and plotting them next to one another, a stacked bar graph plots the various series stacked on top of the previous data range. A *pie chart* compares parts (often percentages) to the whole.

Try to decide what type of graph you are going to create before you define the appropriate ranges. In this project we will examine two types of graphs: a bar graph and a pie chart.

CREATING A BAR GRAPH

We will use a simple bar graph showing sales for January through June for a Sample Company to demonstrate the procedures. Minimum requirements for viewing a graph include choosing a graph type and specifying a range of data to graph.

➤ **To retrieve the SAMPLE worksheet:**

1. Select **/File Retrieve**.

2. Type **SAMPLE** and press ↵.

➤ **To access the Main Graph menu from the READY mode:**

1. Select **/Graph**.

The Main Graph menu should appear in the Control Panel, as shown in the following figure. The Graph Settings box, in the center of the screen, is new to Lotus 1-2-3 Release 2.2 and Release 3. If you have an earlier version of Lotus 1-2-3, you will see just the Control Panel at the top of the screen.

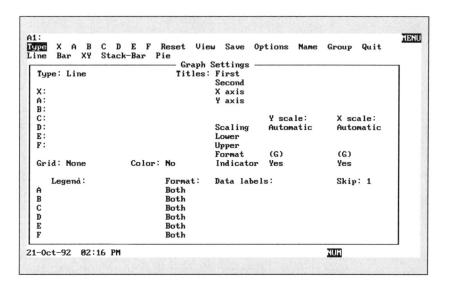

> **To select the graph type:**

1. Select **T**ype.

   The menu containing graph type options should appear in the Control Panel, as shown in the following figure.

```
A1: [W25] 'SAMPLE COMPANY                                              MENU
Line  Bar  XY  Stack-Bar  Pie
Line graph
```

2. Select **B**ar.

   You should see the Main Graph menu reappear in the Control Panel. The Main Graph menu is home base while you are using the graphics portion of Lotus 1-2-3, and it often reappears during the development of a single graph.

> **To select the first series of data to be plotted (out of six possible data series A, B, C, D, E, and F) and indicate the range on the worksheet where the sales figures for January through June are stored:**

1. Select **A** from the Main Graph menu.

2. Type **B9..G9** and press ↵.

Once the location of the first data series is specified (monthly sales in this example), the Main Graph menu reappears on the screen.

> **To view the graph just created:**

1. Select **V**iew.

   Check that your screen matches the one shown in the following figure.

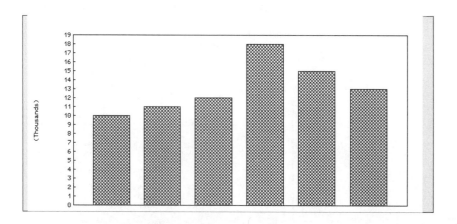

2. Press any key to restore the Main Graph menu.

   If you quit the Main Graph menu and make a change to a graphed figure while in the READY mode, you can press the F10 (GRAPH) key and immediately see the change in the graph. F10 toggles between READY mode and the current graph. A beep sounds if no graph exists. Do not make a change to the data at this time.

ENHANCING A GRAPH

The graph you have just created is too plain to use for most business applications. However, Lotus 1-2-3 offers numerous options for enhancing the graph.

TITLES AND SCALE

One option, *Titles*, permits two labels at the top of the graph, one along the X-axis and one along the Y-axis. Another option, *Scale*, allows you to manually change the upper and/or lower values of the scale initially set by Lotus 1-2-3.

You cannot type labels directly onto a graph. A label is added to a graph by selecting an option from the menu and typing the label, or entering a cell range where the label is located. To demonstrate this concept, you will add titles to the Monthly Sales bar graph and raise the upper Y-axis scale to 20000, so that the bar for April will not be as close to the top border of the graph as it is in the previous figure.

➤ **To access the Graph Options menu and dress up a graph:**

1. Access the READY mode and select /Graph, if the Main Graph menu is not already on the screen.

2. Select Options.

The Graph Options menu should appear in the Control Panel, as shown in the following figure.

```
A1: [W25] 'SAMPLE COMPANY                                              MENU
Legend Format Titles Grid Scale Color B&W Data-Labels Quit
Create legends for data ranges
─────────────────── Graph Settings ───────────────────
```

➤ **To add titles and change the upper Y-axis scale of the current graph:**

1. Select Titles First.

2. Type **SAMPLE COMPANY** and press ↵.

3. Select Titles Second.

4. Type **MONTHLY SALES** and press ↵.

5. Select Titles X-Axis.

6. Type **SALES MONTH** and press ↵.

7. Select Titles Y-Axis.

8. Type **DOLLARS** and press ↵.

9. Select Scale Y–Scale Manual Upper.

10. Type **20000** and press ↵.

11. Select **Q**uit to exit the scale submenu.

12. Press **Q**uit to exit the options submenu.

13. Select **V**iew from the Main Graph menu.

    Check that your graph matches the one shown in the following figure.

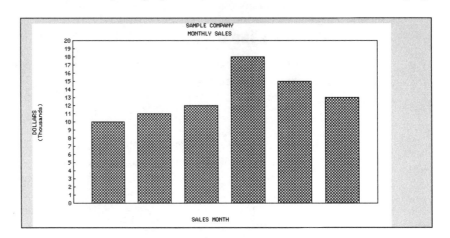

14. Press any key to restore the Main Graph menu.

X-LABELS AND GRID

The **X** choice on the Main Graph menu has two uses: to enter one data series in an XY graph, and add labels below the X-axis on a line, bar, or stacked bar graph or around a pie chart. The **G**rid choice on the Main Graph menu is for adding horizontal and/or vertical background lines to a graph.

To demonstrate these concepts, set a *horizontal grid* and use the monthly headings in row 7 of the SAMPLE file to add X-labels to the current graph.

➤ **To set the horizontal grid:**

1. Select **O**ptions from the Main Graph menu.

2. Select **G**rid.

3. Select **H**orizontal.

4. Select **Q**uit to exit the options submenu.

➤ **To specify labels under the X-axis of the graph and view the enhanced graph:**

1. Select **X** from the Main Graph menu.

2. Type **B7..G7** and press ⏎ to specify monthly headings as labels under the X-axis of the graph.

3. Select **V**iew from the Main Graph menu.

    Check that your graph matches the one shown in the following figure.

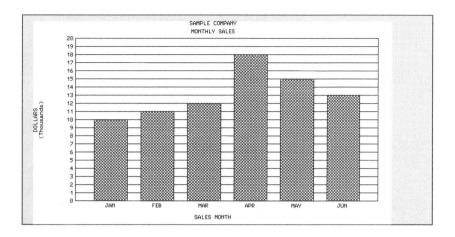

Specification of the X data series and specifying the months in cells B7..G7 resulted in the months being used as labels under the X-axis at the bottom of the graph.

Notice how the horizontal lines on the graph aid reading the scale on the Y-axis.

4.   Press any key to restore the Main Graph menu.

STORING A GRAPH AND GRAPH SETTINGS

Lotus 1-2-3 has two types of storage operations connected with its graphics capability. The command **/Graph Save** stores a graph on disk as a **.PIC** extension file for printing through the PrintGraph program. You cannot change any figure in a graph that has been saved for printing.

The command **/Graph Name Create** stores the graph settings within the worksheet from which the data is drawn, so that when that worksheet is retrieved, the graph may be viewed again as the current graph. Since only the graph settings (type, ranges, titles, etc.) are stored, the numbers and any options reflected in the graph may be altered when the associated worksheet is retrieved. **Name Create** produces an invisible change to the worksheet. You must save the worksheet itself with a **File Save** command once you quit the graphing session.

Save the newly created bar graph for printing and save the graph settings to the worksheet. Once the graph has been saved, it can be printed at any time or transported by disk to another system and then printed.

➤ **To save the current graph as the picture file DEMOBAR.PIC:**

1.   Select **S**ave from the Main Graph menu.

2.   Type **DEMOBAR** and press ↵ when prompted to "Enter graph file name:."

To enter the file name, type the new name. However, if the file name already exists on disk, you will see it in a list of file names in the Control Panel. Highlight the file name and press ↵. The light on the data disk drive will come on to indicate that the file DEMOBAR.PIC is being stored.

➤ To save the current graph settings in the worksheet under the graph name DEMOBAR:

1. Select **N**ame **C**reate from the Main Graph menu.

2. Type **DEMOBAR** and press ⏎ at the "Enter graph name:" prompt.

   Check that your screen matches the one shown in the following figure.

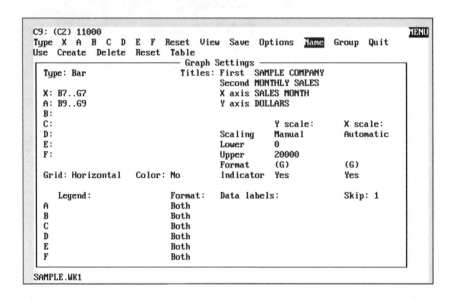

When using the /**G**raph **N**ame command, you see no activity on the data disk drive (the disk drive light does not come on to indicate that files are being saved or stored) because no separate file is created. These settings are stored as part of the worksheet.

To retrieve any graph for which the specifications were stored in the worksheet, select the command **G**raph **N**ame **U**se and specify the appropriate name.

CREATING A PIE CHART

A pie chart is a unique type of graph that is useful in displaying a single data series only. Enter the data range to be graphed under the A data series choice on the Main Graph menu.

Lotus 1-2-3 carries over options used in the most recent graph unless you execute a partial or total graph reset. You will next graph the previous bar graph of Monthly Sales as a pie chart.

➤ To create the pie graph of SAMPLE COMPANY's monthly sales:

1. Access the Main Graph menu.

2. Select **T**ype **P**ie **V**iew.

   Check that your screen matches the pie chart shown in the following figure. The data ranges and titles at the top carry over from the previous bar graph.

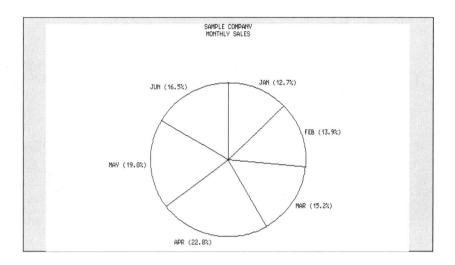

3.   Press any key to restore the Main Graph menu.

➤ **To save the pie chart settings for subsequent retrieval to the screen:**

1.   Select **N**ame **C**reate from the Main Graph menu.

2.   Type **PIE** and press ⏎ to store the graph settings as part of your worksheet.

➤ **To save the pie chart for subsequent printing:**

1.   Select **S**ave from the Main Graph menu.

2.   Type **PIE** and press ⏎ to store the graph as a separate picture file with a .PIC extension.

➤ **To exit the Graph mode and return to the READY mode:**

1.   Select **Q**uit from the Main Graph menu.

➤ **To save the current worksheet to disk, including named graphs:**

1.   Select /**F**ile **S**ave.

2.   Press ⏎ to accept SAMPLE as the name of the file to update.

3.   Select **R**eplace.

Remember to save the worksheet file itself, as you just did in this procedure, after every graphing session. Otherwise, all named graphs will be lost except the last one stored.

PRINTING A GRAPH

Lotus 1-2-3 provides a separate program called PrintGraph to produce graphs on paper. Release 2.2 users can also print with Allways, a desktop publishing add-in packaged with the program. Release 3 users can print a graph from within the Main menu system.

To print graphs, you must have used the /Graph Save command to store the graph in a .PIC extension file, have a printer capable of producing graphics, and have access to the instructions to print the graph. The following figure shows the PrintGraph option on the Lotus 1-2-3 Access System. You see the Access System screen if you type **LOTUS** instead of **123** to load the Lotus 1-2-3 program from the operating system prompt.

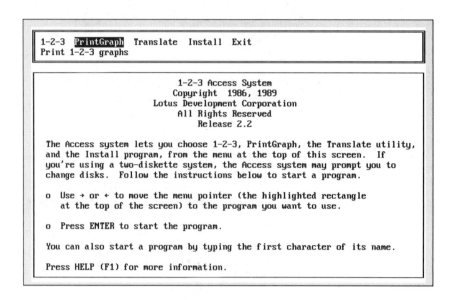

You can also set the current directory to your program files and type **PGRAPH** from the operating system prompt to access the initial PrintGraph screen shown in the next figure.

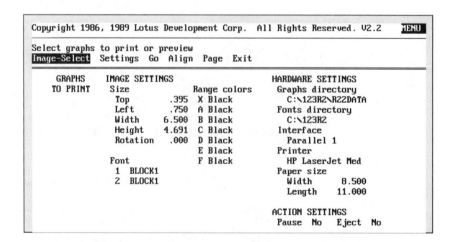

Take a few moments to study the organization of the initial screen. The large area beneath double horizontal lines is the PrintGraph Status screen. Selections made from the first two menu options are reflected in the Status screen. For example, the **I**mage-Select option allows you to specify one or more graphs to print. When you first access this program, the area beneath the GRAPHS TO PRINT column is blank. Use the **S**ettings option to specify three

IMAGE SETTINGS, five HARDWARE SETTINGS, and two ACTION SET-TINGS to control the printer.

The following exercise for printing a graph assumes that the hardware settings (location of graphs, location of print fonts, type of printer, specific printer, and paper size) are correct for your system. After selecting a graph image to print, you can specify the size and rotation of the graph, set one font (print style) for the top title and another for other text in the graph, and set colors if you have a color printer or plotter. You cannot, however, alter the content of the graph.

➤ To preview and then select a graph for printing:

1. Access the PrintGraph program.

2. Select **Image-Select**.

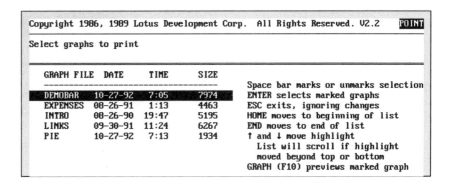

Instructions for selecting and previewing a graph from the list of .PIC extension files on the left side of the status area are provided on the right side. If the DEMOBAR and PIE graphs you created do not appear, check that the graphs directory is correct and that you did use **/G**raph Save to create the required .PIC extension files.

3. Highlight DEMOBAR and press the space bar to mark the graph for selection with a # symbol.

4. Press F10 to preview the graph, allowing you to verify that the correct graph was selected.

5. Press any key, such as the space bar or Esc, to restore the Graph Selection screen.

6. Press ↵ to complete the selection of marked graphs and restore the Main PrintGraph menu.

➤ To select one of the default graph sizes:

1. Notice in the status area the default SIZE settings that produce a half-page graph on 8.5 by 11-inch paper at zero rotation.

2. Select **Settings Image Size**.

```
Copyright 1986, 1989 Lotus Development Corp.  All Rights Reserved. V2.2  MENU

Size graph for full page automatically
Full  Half  Manual  Quit
```

3. Select **F**ull.

    Notice the changes in size specification in the status area, including a 90-degree change in rotation. If you prefer, you can select Manual to set your own size specifications.

4. Select **Q**uit to restore the Image menu.

➤ **To select the print style for the first title line in your graph:**

1. Select **F**ont.

2. Select **1** to specify a font for the first-line graph title.

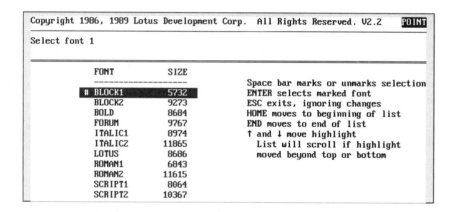

```
Copyright 1986, 1989 Lotus Development Corp.  All Rights Reserved. V2.2  POINT

Select font 1


           FONT      SIZE
                                    Space bar marks or unmarks selection
        # BLOCK1     5732           ENTER selects marked font
          BLOCK2     9273           ESC exits, ignoring changes
          BOLD       8684           HOME moves to beginning of list
          FORUM      9767           END moves to end of list
          ITALIC1    8974           ↑ and ↓ move highlight
          ITALIC2    11865            List will scroll if highlight
          LOTUS      8686             moved beyond top or bottom
          ROMAN1     6843
          ROMAN2     11615
          SCRIPT1    8064
          SCRIPT2    10367
```

3. Press the space bar to unmark the default font selection BLOCK1 and mark another font of your choice.

4. Press ⏎ to select the marked font and restore the Image menu.

    The font you selected should appear as both Font 1 and Font 2 in the status area. If you prefer another style for the other titles and labels in the graph, repeat the previous steps, but select **2** in step 2.

5. Select **Q**uit **Q**uit to restore the Main PrintGraph menu.

During the time a graph prints, the mode indicator in the upper-right corner flashes WAIT, indicating that you cannot use the computer until the current print job is completed. Printing graphs is a very slow process.

➤ **To complete the print process for DEMOBAR.PIC:**

1. Check that a graphics printer is available, the paper is correctly positioned in the printer, and the printer is on-line.

2. Select **A**lign.

3. Select **G**o and wait until the graph prints.

4. Select **P**age.

➤ **To select the graph PIE.PIC for printing:**

1. Select **I**mage-Select from the PrintGraph program.

2. Highlight PIE and press the space bar to mark the graph for selection with a # symbol.

3. Press ⏎ to complete the selection of marked graphs and restore the Main PrintGraph menu.

➤ **To complete the print process for PIE.PIC and exit PrintGraph:**

1. Check that a graphics printer is available, the paper is positioned in the printer, and the printer is on-line.

2. Select **A**lign.

3. Select **G**o and wait until the graph prints.

4. Select **P**age.

5. Select **E**xit **Y**es.

This concludes the hands-on exercises for the graphics portion of Lotus 1-2-3. You created only two of five types of graphs and you used only a few of the many graph options. Refer to the complete list of Graph menu options in the Command Reference section at the end of this module and experiment with other graph types and enhancements.

SUMMARY

- Lotus 1-2-3 offers five types of graphs: line, bar, XY, stacked bar, and pie.

- Line graphs are especially suited to show changes in data over time, while bar graphs are often used to compare sets of data.

- A stacked bar graph is similar to a bar graph except that multiple data ranges are graphed one on top of the other as compared to side-by-side.

- An XY graph illustrates the relationship between two or more sets of data.

- A pie chart expresses each data item graphed as a percentage of the total graphed range. Only one set of data can be graphed.

- Two steps are required to create a graph: selecting a graph type and defining one or more data ranges.

- A **V**iew option on the Main Graph menu allows you to frequently display the graph you are creating.

- A variety of enhancements to graphs can be made by invoking options, such as titles, labels, background grid, and changes in scale.

- If data in a graphed range changes, the results of the change can be seen immediately in the graph.

- A graph can be saved as a .PIC extension file and printed with the PrintGraph program.

- For viewing a graph during a subsequent work session, you can select **N**ame **C**reate from the Main Graph menu to store the graph specifications in the worksheet, much like a **R**ange **N**ame is stored in a worksheet. After exiting the Main Graph menu but before exiting Lotus 1-2-3, execute a **F**ile **S**ave command to update the worksheet to include any new graph specifications.

- Lotus 1-2-3 provides a separate program called PrintGraph to produce graphs on paper. Release 2.2 users can also print with Allways, a desktop publishing add-in packaged with the program. Release 3 users can initiate printing from within the Main menu system.

KEY TERMS

.PIC	line graph	stacked bar graph
bar graph	pie chart	Titles
horizontal grid	Scale	XY graph

STUDY QUESTIONS

TRUE/FALSE

1. To create a graph, you need only specify the type of graph and the data labels to be used. **T**   **F**

2. Enhancing a graph with titles, labels, and grid lines makes the graph more readable. **T**   **F**

3. Graphs that are to be printed must be saved using the **/G**raph **S**ave option. **T**   **F**

4. Graphs saved using the **/G**raph **S**ave option can be edited after they have been printed. **T**   **F**

5. The current graph can be viewed from the READY mode. **T**   **F**

6. You can set a horizontal grid or a vertical grid on a graph, but you cannot set both grids for a single graph. **T**   **F**

7. Lotus 1-2-3 automatically sets the scale on a graph based on the values in the graphed data ranges. **T**   **F**

8. When more than one graph is created for a worksheet, only the last graph created can be viewed in the next work session unless the settings for the other graphs were saved using the **/G**raph **N**ame **C**reate command. **T**   **F**

9. You are limited to two title specifications on a graph. **T**   **F**

10. Using PrintGraph, you can print graphs in two sizes only: full and half. **T**   **F**

FILL IN THE BLANKS

1. The minimum specifications necessary to create a graph are the graph type and one _____.

2. A pie chart can display _Single_ data range(s).

3. A graph type in which data ranges are graphed one on top of another is called a _Stacked bar_ graph.

4. Horizontal and vertical lines added to a graph are called _____ lines.

5. The numbers that Lotus 1-2-3 automatically displays along the vertical axis of the graph depict the _____ of the graph.

6. Data labels added to the bottom of the graph are specified using the _____ data range.

7. Graphs that are to be printed must be stored to disk using the /Graph __Save__ option.

8. To see your graph while working in the Graph mode, select _____.

9. To see the current graph from the READY mode, press _____.

10. Type _____ from the operating system prompt to access the PrintGraph program.

SHORT ANSWER

1. What effect does a change in graphed data in the worksheet have on the graph?

2. Describe two applications for which you might want to create a graph.

3. Describe how to add data labels to the X-axis of a bar graph.

4. Describe some of the options Lotus 1-2-3 provides to enhance the appearance of a graph.

5. Discuss reasons why you might want to change the scale of a graph.

REVIEW EXERCISES

1. Retrieve the SAMPLE worksheet.

2. Display the DEMOBAR graph.

3. Access the Main Graph menu, change the graph type of DEMOBAR to Line, and view the graph.

4. Save the current line graph as LINE.PIC.

5. Save the graph specifications for the line graph in the worksheet.

6. Access the Main Graph menu, change the graph type to Bar, add a B data range for January to June Net Income figures, and view the graph.

7. Save the current comparative bar graph as TWOBAR.PIC.

8. Save the graph specifications for the comparative bar graph in the worksheet.

9. Save the SAMPLE worksheet.

10. Print the comparative bar graph TWOBAR.PIC and the line graph LINE.PIC.

COMPETENCY TESTING

- Review the Topic Objectives to ensure you have mastered all skills listed.

- Ask your Class Assistant to check off:

  - Your Project work (the printed directory listing mentioned above in the Practice Exercises section, the worksheet SAMPLE, and the two graph printouts).

  - Your completed True/False and Fill in the Blanks exercises.

  - Your completed Review Exercises (two graph printouts and your TDL).

- Ask your Class Assistant to see the **Graphing Data**:

  - **Project Sample Sheet** to compare your work against the samples.

  - **True/False and Fill in the Blanks Correct Answer Sheet** to compare your answers against the correct ones.

  - **Review Exercises Sample Answer Sheet** to compare your work against it.

COMPETENCY TEST PREPARATION AND SUMMARY

COMPETENCY TEST PREPARATION

Congratulations! You have now completed all the work in the *BASIS* Computer Applications Lotus 1-2-3 module. All you have to do now is:

- Review the objectives for all topics to ensure you have mastered all the skills for the module.

- Review your notes and practice where necessary.

- Check to make sure you have completed all work necessary to qualify you to attempt the competency test.

- Do the competency test.

 ## MODULE OBJECTIVES

Here is a summary of the objectives for all topics in the module, in alphabetical order:

- Add a legend to a graph.

- Cancel (undo) most recent change (*Note*: Covered in Computer Tutorial *only*).

- Change column width.

  - Change single column.

  - Change global width.

- Change the current directory temporarily.

- Change global defaults.

- Check worksheet status.

- Combine all or part of a worksheet into another worksheet.

  - Expand a worksheet by incorporating existing data from another worksheet.

- Copy or move cell contents.

- Create and enhance a graph (titles, scale, grid).

- Create a pie chart.

- Design a worksheet.

- Display Access System menu (*Note*: Covered in Computer Tutorial *only*).

- Display name of current worksheet on screen (in place of clock display).

- Edit data.

- Edit or erase cell contents.
- Edit formulas.
- Enter labels, numbers, formulas, and functions.
- Erase files from disk.
- Exit Lotus.
- Exit to DOS temporarily.
- Extract a portion of a worksheet to a disk file.
- Format a range containing formulas as text.
- Identify a graph's type: line, bar, XY, stacked bar, or pie.
- Insert and delete columns or rows.
- List file names of files stored on disk.
- Move around worksheet (special keys).
- Name cell ranges.
- Perform basic file maintenance tasks.
  - Set directory temporarily.
  - Save current worksheet.
  - Erase worksheet and begin creating a new worksheet.
  - Retrieve a file from disk.
- Print a graph using PrintGraph (preview, select size and style).
- Print worksheet contents cell by cell (cell contents and cell attributes).
- Remove numbers from a worksheet, retaining labels and formulas.
  - Create a reusable worksheet by removing only numeric data.
- Retrieve a worksheet.
- Save current worksheet, including named graphs.
- Save a graph as a .PIC file that can be printed ("save" the graph).
- Save, print, and erase current worksheet.
- Select an appropriate graph type.
- Select option from a menu.
  - Access the Lotus 1-2-3 menu system.
- Specify number formats (range or global).
- Start Lotus 1-2-3.
- Store graph specifications within the associated worksheet ("name" the graph).
- Switch between automatic and manual recalculation.
- Understand the worksheet screen.
- Use @function to date stamp a worksheet (@NOW).
- Use @SUM.

- Use formulas to link worksheets.

- Use function keys.

  - Ten function keys.

  - Edit keys.

- Use and/or identify Lotus 1-2-3's set of built-in @functions (@SUM, @DATE, @NOW, @COUNT, @ROUND, @INT, @AVG, @MIN, @MAX, @PMT).

- Use Lotus 1-2-3's on-line help facility.

- Use prefix characters to align labels within a range of cells.

- Use range name in formulas.

- Use relative and absolute cell addressing.

- Use "what if" analysis (*Note*: Covered in Computer Tutorial *only*).

- View global default status

- View graph on screen.

- View two portions of a worksheet.

  - Freeze titles.

  - Use worksheet window.

COMPUTER TUTORIAL

If necessary, glance through computer tutorials. The **Review** and **Important Concepts** sections at the end of each tutorial are a good review. Also, if you haven't already tried them, do the exercises (**I** from the **Advanced** section).

COMPETENCY TESTING

To qualify for the Lotus 1-2-3 module competency test, you must have completed all the work outlined in the Practice Exercises sections of each topic in the module, and have had all of that work checked off as summarized in the Competency Testing sections. For more information about module competency tests, consult your *BASIS* System Administrator and/or your *BASIS* **Student Manual**.

Double check now to make sure that you have all work completed and checked off:

TOPIC	REQUIRED WORK
Introduction to Lotus 1-2-3	❏ True/False Exercises ❏ Fill in the Blanks Exercises
Creating a Worksheet	❏ Project work (printout of SAMPLE) ❏ True/False Exercises ❏ Fill in the Blanks Exercises ❏ Review Exercises work (printout of PER-SPROP and TDL)
Modifying and Document-ing a Worksheet	❏ Project work (SAMPLE and first direc-tory listing) ❏ True/False Exercises ❏ Fill in the Blanks Exercises ❏ Review Exercises work (PERSPROP, two printouts and TDL)
Managing the Environ-ment and Files	❏ Project work (in-process check or direc-tory listing) ❏ True/False Exercises ❏ Fill in the Blanks Exercises ❏ Review Exercises work (in-process check or directory listing; TDL)
Working with Multiple Worksheets	❏ Project work (directory listing; six work-sheets) ❏ True/False Exercises ❏ Fill in the Blanks Exercises ❏ Review Exercises work (TOTHOURS, TOTHRS2, and your TDL)
Graphing Data	❏ Project work (directory listing; SAM-PLE, and two graph printouts) ❏ True/False Exercises ❏ Fill in the Blanks Exercises ❏ Review Exercises work (two graph printouts and TDL)

SUMMARY

We hope that you have enjoyed your *BASIS* Computer Applications Lotus 1-2-3 module. This text will serve as a useful reference for you in the future, and the computer tutorials are often helpful for a quick review.

To further develop your Lotus skills, we highly recommend the following material from the Novice and Advanced computer tutorials listed below (*Note*: The following is *not* required for the *BASIS* Lotus module competency test).

SECTION		NOTES
Novice	**E Sort Data**	The /Data Sort command allows you to alphabetize or numerically sort information in a range of cells according to data in one or two columns in that range.
Advanced	**G Create macros**	If you regularly enter the same series of keystrokes, macros can save you a lot of time. A macro is just a series of keystrokes stored in a cell as a label. When you execute the macro, the keystrokes are played in sequence automatically.

COMMAND REFERENCES

Worksheet Commands

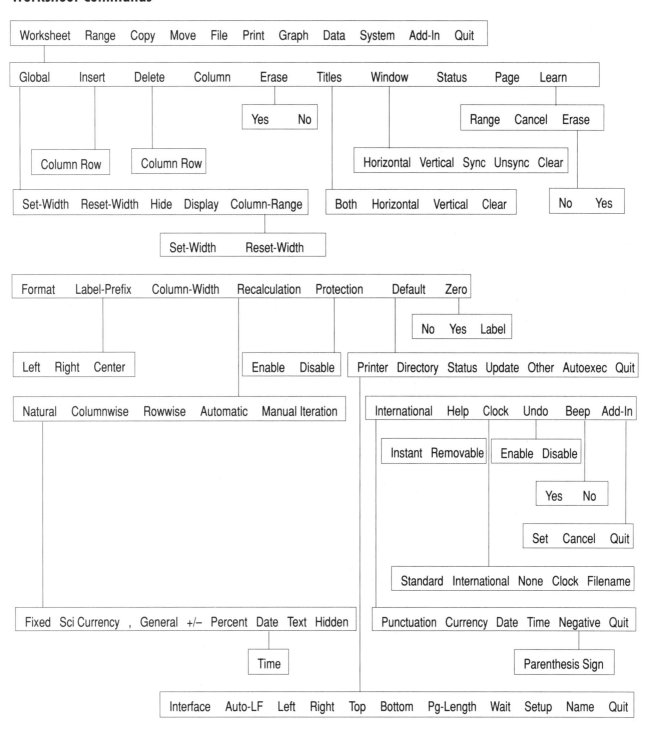

Range Commands

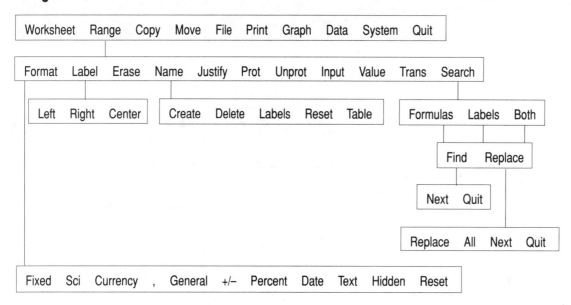

Copy and Move Commands

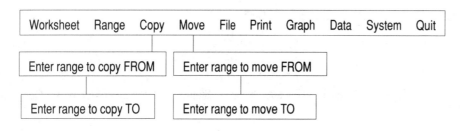

File Commands

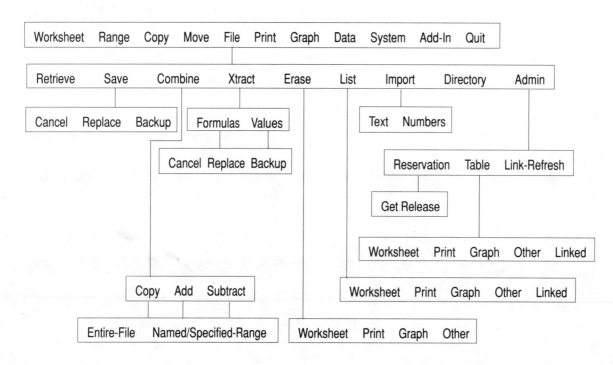

Print Commands

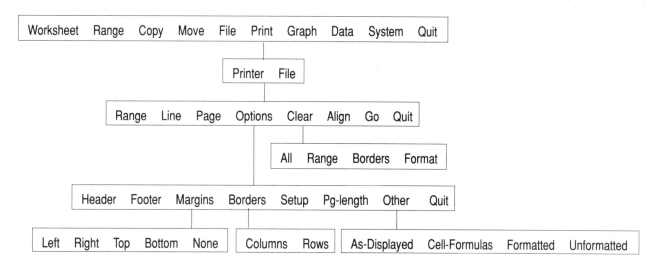

Graph Commands

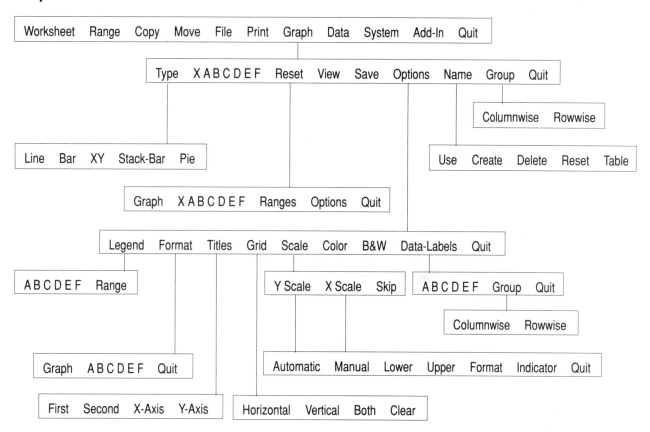

Data Commands

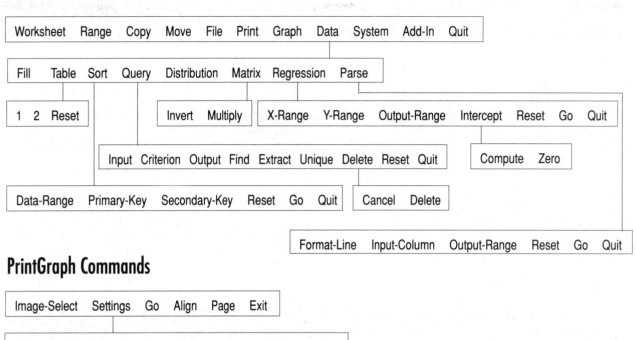

| Worksheet | Range | Copy | Move | File | Print | Graph | Data | System | Add-In | Quit |

| Fill | Table | Sort | Query | Distribution | Matrix | Regression | Parse |

| 1 | 2 | Reset |

| Invert | Multiply |

| X-Range | Y-Range | Output-Range | Intercept | Reset | Go | Quit |

| Input | Criterion | Output | Find | Extract | Unique | Delete | Reset | Quit |

| Compute | Zero |

| Data-Range | Primary-Key | Secondary-Key | Reset | Go | Quit |

| Cancel | Delete |

| Format-Line | Input-Column | Output-Range | Reset | Go | Quit |

PrintGraph Commands

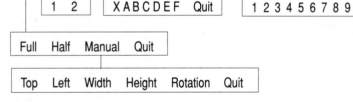

| Image-Select | Settings | Go | Align | Page | Exit |

| Image | Hardware | Action | Save | Reset | Quit |

| Pause | Eject | Quit |

| Graphs-Directory | Fonts-Directory | Interface | Printer | Size-Paper | Quit |

| Size | Font | Range-Colors | Quit |

| 1 2 3 4 5 6 7 8 |

| Length | Width | Quit |

| 1 | 2 |

| X A B C D E F | Quit |

| 1 2 3 4 5 6 7 8 9 |

| Full | Half | Manual | Quit |

| Top | Left | Width | Height | Rotation | Quit |

Add-In Commands

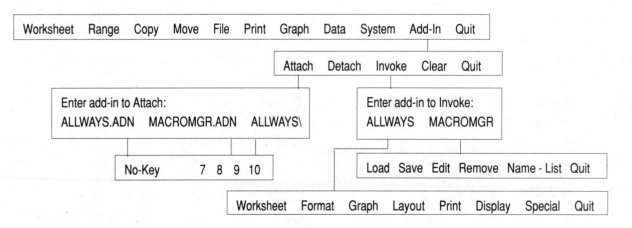

| Worksheet | Range | Copy | Move | File | Print | Graph | Data | System | Add-In | Quit |

| Attach | Detach | Invoke | Clear | Quit |

| Enter add-in to Attach: |
| ALLWAYS.ADN   MACROMGR.ADN   ALLWAYS\ |

| Enter add-in to Invoke: |
| ALLWAYS   MACROMGR |

| No-Key | 7 | 8 | 9 | 10 |

| Load | Save | Edit | Remove | Name - List | Quit |

| Worksheet | Format | Graph | Layout | Print | Display | Special | Quit |

GLOSSARY FOR LOTUS 1-2-3

$ A symbol that, when placed before the column letter or row number of a cell address, causes the coordinates of a copied cell to be the same in the target location as the source location. *See also* absolute address.

absolute address A cell address that, when copied or moved, does not change.

align To position label contents within a cell left, right, or centered.

anchor To lock in the upper-left corner of a range when specifying a range by pointing.

ascending order The arrangement of records in numeric and alphabetic order.

bar graph A graph that depicts up to six data ranges as bars above a horizontal axis.

bug An error in a macro.

cell An area on the worksheet that can contain labels, values, or formulas. Cells are arranged in rows and columns similar to a sheet of ledger paper. Each cell falls at the intersection of a row and a column.

cell address The location of a cell within the worksheet defined by row and column coordinates. Rows are identified by numbers and columns by letters. For example, the upper-leftmost cell on the worksheet is A1, representing the intersection of column A and row 1. The cell address appears in the upper-left corner of the screen.

cell attributes User-specified characteristics including cell width and format for numeric display.

cell pointer A highlight bar indicating the cell where data can be entered or edited. The current cell pointer position displays in the upper-left corner of the Control Panel.

closed macro A macro that completes its stored instructions without user intervention.

column Cells arranged vertically down a worksheet and identified by a column letter; in a database, a column is equivalent to a field of data.

combination keys Two or more keys activated by pressing the first key and holding it down while pressing the second key and then releasing both keys.

command sequence A series of Lotus 1-2-3 menu selections that perform a specific action.

context-sensitive A Help mode that displays information about the current operation.

copy To duplicate a block of text at another location in a worksheet.

criteria range A range of cells that contains one or more search conditions.

Currency format A cell format that displays values with commas, a decimal point, and a dollar sign.

database The "3" in Lotus 1-2-3. A database manages data as a file of records stored in a worksheet format. Each row represents a record in the database, and each column represents a field in the records. Several data commands facilitate searching for records, extracting records, creating tables of information, and developing frequency distribution.

data range A range containing records to be sorted.

debug To remove errors from a macro.

descending order The arrangement of records in reverse numeric and alphabetic order.

editing The process of adding, changing, and deleting records.

environment Lotus 1-2-3 default settings that control worksheet operations.

erase To delete cell contents, the current worksheet, or files from disk.

ERR A message that appears in a cell when the cell contents are not valid.

exit To discontinue using Lotus 1-2-3 and return to DOS.

extracted record A record that meets specified search conditions during a Data Query Extract operation.

extracting formulas Copying a range of cells to disk as a new worksheet and transferring formulas contained in cells.

extracting ranges Copying a range of cells to disk as a new worksheet.

extracting values Copying a range of cells to disk as a new worksheet and transferring formulas contained in cells as values.

field A group of related characters in a database record—for example, a person's first name.

file A collection of related records stored in a file on disk—for example, a file of stock records containing inventory information.

Fixed format A cell format that displays values showing a fixed number of decimal places.

formula An equation that performs mathematical operations and displays the results in a cell. Formulas may contain math operators, values, cell locations, functions, or other formulas.

function A formula built into Lotus 1-2-3 that performs a specific operation. For example, the @AVG function computes the average of the values contained in a range of cells. There are nearly 100 functions (depending on the version of Lotus 1-2-3 you use) to perform commonly used operations, such as computing averages.

global default A setting that applies to all cells or columns in a worksheet.

graphics The "2" in Lotus 1-2-3. A tool that lets you present your worksheet data as powerful business graphs.

horizontal grid Horizontal background lines on a graph that make the graph more readable.

incoming data Information to be placed in a target area.

incoming range A range of cells being combined into the current worksheet from a worksheet on disk.

input range A specification of a number of records to be searched in a database.

Insert mode Causes newly input characters entered from the keyboard to shift existing text to the right of the current cursor position.

key A field in a database used to sort records into a meaningful sequence.

keyboard macro A collection of keystrokes stored in a worksheet cell(s) that can be executed by typing a single key combination.

keyword A word used in a macro to trigger an executable action.

label Descriptive information in a worksheet. A label usually begins with a letter; it may not start with any character that is interpreted as a value.

label prefix character A character indicating the contents of a label.

line graph A graph that plots data as points on a line and is well-suited to show changes in data over time.

list To view file names stored on disk.

long label A label that exceeds the width of the column in which it is stored. A long label displays into the next adjacent cell on the right if this cell contains no data. When the adjacent cell contains data, the excess of the label is hidden from view. The entire entry can, however, be seen on line 1 of the Control Panel, and will appear on the worksheet if the adjacent cell is erased.

macro library A collection of macro programs stored in a worksheet.

menu bar A menu of choices across the top of the screen; selecting a choice causes a menu to appear.

mixed addresses A combination of relative and absolute cell addresses.

mode indicator The mode Lotus 1-2-3 is performing in at the moment. The current mode is indicated in the upper-right corner of the screen. In the READY mode, you may enter data into the worksheet. In the MENU mode, you may make selections from a menu at the top of the screen.

move To transfer the contents of a range of cells from one location to another in a worksheet.

number Numeric cell contents beginning with numbers 0 through 9 or the characters . + - $ or (.

open macro A macro that pauses or terminates before the task is finished, giving the user an opportunity to include variable information.

output area *See* output range.

output range A range of cells used to store records that meet specified search conditions during a database query.

.PIC A file extension assigned by Lotus 1-2-3 when a graph is saved for printing.

pie chart A graph that plots data in a single data range, as wedges of a pie; the wedges total 100%.

pointing method Making menu selections or specifying ranges by highlighting the desired choice or range, as opposed to typing.

primary key The field controlling the initial order of records being sorted.

printable character Keyboard keys representing characters that can be printed.

query A procedure for accessing selected records from a database.

range One or more cells arranged in a rectangle that can be referenced by specifying the upper-left cell and the lower-right cell.

recalculate To recompute formula results after a change in cells containing numbers, formulas, functions, or cell references. If recalculation is set to Manual, press F9 to recalculate the worksheet.

record A group of related fields in a database; for example, a stock record containing fields of data about an item of furniture in an inventory.

relative address A cell address that, when copied or moved, changes relative to the direction of the move.

retrieve Loading a document from disk into memory for display on your screen.

row Cells arranged horizontally across one line in a worksheet and identified by a number; in a database, a row represents a record.

save Storing a document onto disk.

scale Graduations that appear on the Y-axis (all graph types except pie) and X-axis (XY graph only) to denote the amounts corresponding to graphed data.

search conditions The criteria used to find or extract specific records in a database.

secondary key A field controlling the order of records being sorted within a primary key.

sort To arrange a group of records in a database in ascending or descending order by primary and secondary keys.

source range The range from which data is being moved or copied.

spreadsheet An alternate term for worksheet.

stacked bar graph A graph that plots each range as bars above the previous data range.

status An on-screen report displaying current environment settings related to the worksheet, printer, and directories.

status indicators Indicators at the bottom of the screen that show the default setting for keys such as CapsLock and NumLock.

STEP An option used while debugging macros to slow execution of the macro.

target The range to which data is being moved or copied.

target area A range of cells in the current worksheet that will receive incoming data.

Titles Headings placed at the top of a graph or along the X-axis and Y-axis of a graph.

typing method Making menu selections or specifying ranges by typing the first letter of the desired choice or the range cell references.

value The numeric contents of a cell. Values consist of numbers, formulas, cell addresses, or functions.

"what-if" analysis A powerful calculation tool used in worksheets. Once a formula(s) has been set up for a worksheet, different values can be substituted in various cells, and the effect(s) of these changes can be seen in the outcome values in other cells.

worksheet The "1" in Lotus 1-2-3. The primary Lotus 1-2-3 work surface, made up of cells arranged in 8192 rows and 256 columns. The cells may contain labels, values, or formulas. Each time the contents of a cell are changed, all formulas stored in the worksheet are computed again. A worksheet is often called a spreadsheet.

XY graph A graph that depicts relationships, if any, among plotted data ranges.

INDEX

416-415-9363.